10.60

EVIL
The Shadow Side of Reality

Quadrant
winter 75
vol 8 #2 P21-22

Persona + Marks

P101 - mask of persona

EVIL

The Shadow Side of Reality
by JOHN A. SANFORD

Franklin J Kane

Sept '68

Read May '84

CROSSROAD • NEW YORK

1987

The Crossroad Publishing Company
370 Lexington Avenue, New York, N.Y. 10017

Printed in the United States of America

Library of Congress Cataloging in Publication Data

Sanford, John A
Evil: the shadow side of reality.
Bibliography: p.
1. Good and evil. I. Title.
BJ1401.S26   216   81-625
ISBN 0-8245-0037-7   AACR1
ISBN 0-8245-0526-3 pbk

ACKNOWLEDGMENTS

Excerpt(s) from *The Jerusalem Bible,* copyright © 1966 by Darton, Longman & Todd, Ltd. and Doubleday & Company, Inc. Used by permission of the publisher.

Satprem, *Sri Aurobindo, or the Adventure of Consciousness.* New York, Harper & Row Publishers, 1970. Used by permission.

I want to thank the many persons who have helped me with this manuscript. My special thanks to my friends Robert Johnson and Morton Kelsey, who read this manuscript for me and made many helpful suggestions, and also to Allan Anderson, Ph.D., whose keen insights into the philosophical aspects of the problem of evil were of special help to me in the last chapter. I would also like to thank Helen Macey for her invaluable help in the preparation of this manuscript.

To my good friend, Morton T. Kelsey

Contents

Introduction

For those who espouse the Judaeo–Christian faiths, with their teaching about good intentions, justice, and the loving kindness of God, the presence of evil in the world raises disturbing questions and lies in their religious stomachs like an undigested meal. For others, the reality of evil is, perhaps more than anything else, the roadblock that keeps them from a religious faith and turns them to an attitude of atheism, cynicism, or despair. And of course for all of us evil is a constant threat for it has power to possess and destroy the human soul or extinguish our lives through war, disease, or crime. So evil is a problem that ultimately none of us can avoid, though many people are experts at keeping their heads in the sand, ostrich fashion, as long as they can. This attitude of hiding from evil, however, can no longer be possible when we begin to suffer. Suffering always brings the problem of evil with it, and the problem of evil and the problem of suffering are companions. In this book the focus is more philosophical than pastoral, more aimed at the problem of evil than at the problem of suffering, but the problem of suffering always underlies everything that is said.

Naturally there have been many efforts to deal with the problem of suffering, and innumerable books written on the subject. Why then one more book, especially since I must say from the start that I make no pretense at having solved the problem of evil and do not claim to have made any definitive statement concerning the relationship of evil to God. The answer lies in the unique contribution to the problem that is being made by depth psychology, especially by the Analytical Psychology of C. G. Jung.[1]

When we look at a problem from the perspective of the

1

psychology of the unconscious, it is like looking from the inside out. Imagine looking at a round ball. You would, of course, be looking at the *outside* of the ball. Then imagine that you were very small and were looking at the same ball, but from the *inside*. You would now have an entirely different perspective. This, roughly speaking, is the change of perspective that comes when we view human problems through the eyes of the unconscious. We study the same problems, but they look different than they did before. How the problem of evil looks when seen from the viewpoint of the unconscious has been scarcely touched upon, and the relationship of this psychological insight to Christian lore and biblical teaching has been virtually ignored. I hope this book will help fill the gap.

While the theme that runs throughout the book is the nature of evil as seen from the vantage point of religion and psychology, each chapter is something of a unit in itself. Chapter One deals with the reality of evil, and what is seen as good and what is seen as evil varies with the point of view of the observer, which brings up the question of whether there is also an absolute viewpoint about good and evil. Chapter Two looks for such a viewpoint, beyond that of the particular human being, in mythology. Chapter Three examines the relationship of evil to God in the Old Testament, and in particular how evil in the Old Testament relates to the psychological idea of the "dark side of the Self." The Fourth Chapter turns to the New Testament, with a particular view to Jesus' understanding of evil. Chapter Five goes into the important matter of the Shadow, a unique contribution of Analytical Psychology to our understanding of the problem evil poses to human consciousness, and Chapters Six and Seven continue the exploration of the shadow problem by examining the differing views of Jesus and Paul, and by a study of Stevenson's instructive novelette *The Strange Case of Dr. Jekyll and Mr. Hyde.* Chapter Eight sees how post-biblical Christian and Jewish mythology throw light on the psychological meaning behind the idea of the devil.

The last chapter, which compares Christian and Jungian thoughts regarding evil and its relationship to God, requires special mention. In many ways Jungian psychology corroborates and enlivens the Christian point of view. In fact, Analytical Psychology claims to be the successor to medieval alchemy, which is nothing other than the mystical companion to the Christianity of the Church. This natural companionship of the two disciplines, however, has often come to grief with regard to the problem of evil. Jung's view can appear to the Christian point of view as a dangerous espousal of the principle of evil. On the other hand, the Christian attitude, from the vantage point of psychology, has been hotly criticized as exposing mankind to the power of evil because it seems to assert that evil has no substance in its own right. This difference of opinion apparently almost destroyed one of Jung's deepest friendships, that with Father Victor White, a Roman Catholic theologian who interested himself in Jungian psychology back in the days when hardly anyone knew about it, and who became a close friend of Dr. Jung. Yet as the years went on their relationship almost came to grief because the two differed in the way they perceived the relationship of evil to God. It was salvaged only when, in the final days of Victor White's life, the positive feeling of the two men came through to overcome their philosophical differences. It is, I think, fitting that this book concludes with an examination of this vexing problem, in the hope that this may help create a common ground between psychology and Christianity where the difficult problem of evil may be more amicably discussed.

I once saw a film [2] in which a disillusioned crusader has returned home and longs to know about God. He hears of a witch who is being burned at the stake and finds her just before the flames are going to engulf her. "Can you tell me where I can find the devil?" he asks. "Why do you wish to find the devil?" the doomed girl replies. "Because maybe the devil can tell me about God," the soul-sick knight answers. Hopefully we will be able to find God more directly in our lives and not undergo the torment of the disillusioned crusader, but the fact remains that if we can gain a deeper insight into the nature of and reasons for evil, we may also learn more about the nature of God. It is with this hope that this book has been written.

Notes

[1] Henceforth in this book, when I speak of psychology I am referring specifically to the psychology of C. G. Jung, which is properly called Analytical Psychology.

[2] I believe it was from the Swedish film *The Seventh Seal.* Quotations are from memory and may not be exact.

CHAPTER ONE

Ego-Centered and Divine Perspectives on Evil

One summer I planted a vigorous young squash plant in a large planter tub in my front yard. The plant flourished and the large, strong leaves were as decorative as any flower in my garden. It gave me a lot of satisfaction to go out each morning and admire my plant, and much pleasure when I saw the squashes beginning to form at the base of the beautiful yellow flowers. But one morning I saw an ominous sight: small blotches of a whitish, powdery substance covered some of the leaves. Each day the whitish substance on my plant increased, as the powdery mildew slowly but surely took over the plant, robbing it of its strength, drying up its fruit, and turning the beautiful green of the leaves to a sickly pale color. There was nothing that I could do; no remedy I tried could cure the plant of its ailment, and in time there was nothing to do but pull up the plant and discard it.

The same year I had some glorious tomato plants. There is nothing more lush and alive than a healthy tomato plant, and no fruit more tasteful, nourishing, and beautiful than a tomato that has been ripened on the vine. But one day as I inspected my plants I found one that had been neatly severed at the base. Where there had once been a healthy plant, now there was a dead remnant and a hole in the ground. The next day it happened again, and again the day after that. Gardeners among you know that a gopher had invaded my garden and was making short work of my tomatoes. This time I was more successful in helping my plants as the thieving gopher fell prey to one of my traps.

I regarded the powdery mildew that had destroyed my squash

plant as an evil, and the gopher, too, I regarded as an evil that had to be destroyed. I do not know how the powdery mildew felt, but the gopher, no doubt, felt that what it was doing was good and that *I*, and my traps, were evil. What I regarded as evil, the gopher regarded as good, and the other way around.

So the first thing we must face with regard to evil is that from a human point of view it seems to be relative to the viewpoint of the observer, so that what may be regarded as good for one creature is evil for another. Nicholas Berdyaev, for example, speaks of a Hottentot who defined evil by saying, "It is *good* if I steal some-b ɔdy else's wife and *bad* if my wife is stolen from me." [1]

In the years 1616–1619 a frightful epidemic swept through what is now New England decimating the native Indian population. Evidently the disease (probably smallpox) had entered the area from a visit by an English slaver, and the Indians, not used to the white man's diseases, had no immunity against it. In 1620 the Pilgrim Fathers, so idealized in our schoolbooks, arrived to permanently colonize the land and found it conveniently emptied of its native population. Historian William Brandon writes, "The Churchly colonists exulted, with reverence, over the frightful epidemic of 1616–1619 that had cleared so many heathen from the path of the Chosen People." Brandon cites one Puritan divine who spoke of "The Wonderful Preparation the Lord Christ by His Providence Wrought for His People's Abode in this Western World." This man of God went on to speak with particular satisfaction of how the plague had swept away "chiefly young men and children, the very seeds of increase." Another divine observed that "in this, the wondrous wisedome and love of God is shewne, by sending to the place his Minister (that is, death), to sweepe away . . . the Salvages. . . ." [2]

And yet we can imagine that what seemed such a good and divinely inspired event to the Puritans seemed like a terrible evil to the unfortunate Indians, and while the Puritan divines could ascribe the epidemic to the love and providence of God without any apparent qualm of conscience, we, if we have any feeling at all, are shocked at their self-centered and arrogant attitude and sense evil in their very words. (This is a good time to point out the distinction between what might be called "moral" evil and "natural" evil. The powdery mildew that destroyed my squash plant is an example of natural evil, as are events like earthquakes, destructive floods or epidemics. Moral evil comes from what appears to be evil motives in the hearts of mankind.)

The notion of the relativity of good and evil is not new. The ancient Chinese philosopher Chu Hsi, for instance, whose reflections occurred so long ago that no one is sure exactly when he lived, taught that good and evil have no existence in themselves, but are terms applied to things according to their advantage or injury to oneself or to mankind. "Nature itself," Chu Hsi taught, "is beyond good and evil and ignores our egoistic terminology." [3] The same thought is reflected in Hamlet's words when he says to Rosencrantz, "There is nothing either good or bad, but thinking makes it so." [4]

Theology, however, is not content with the humanist view that what is good and what is evil is always relative and only to be decided by the viewpoint of a human observer. For if this is so, then there is no fundamental moral basis to life or the universe, nor is there any moral order to curb mankind from its egocentric and destructively self–serving ambitions. In war, for instance, each side routinely claims God to be on its side. Even Hitler's Germany was convinced that its cause was righteous, though it was apparent to the rest of the world that Nazi Germany was possessed by evil. Somewhere, religion cries out, there *is* a God Who has what might be called an Absolute or Objective standard by which what is good and what is evil is truly to be measured.

Psychology helps us here with its distinction between the *ego* and the *Self*. The ego can be defined as the center of the conscious personality. It is the "I" part of us with which we are consciously identified, the part of us that does the willing, choosing, and suffering in life, and that has a certain continuity of memory, so that when we say, "*I* did this" or "*I* did that" we are thinking of the ego. The Self is the name psychology gives to the center of the *total personality*. (For this reason the Self is sometimes also called the *Center*.) Therefore the Self is another name for the whole person, the larger personality that includes, but is greater than, the ego, and which, in religious language, might be called the "Christ–personality."

When the ego views life and its own concerns only from its own vantage point, we speak of "egocentricity," and we know that the egocentric viewpoint is always narrow and limited. The process of psychotherapy attempts to alter the egocentric standpoint by introducing the viewpoint of the Self. This results, when it can be done, in a shift of the conscious standpoint from an egocentric point of view to the larger point of view of the Self, with salutary results. Clearly the goals of personality development of psychology and religion are, at this point at least, identical, since both strive to relate a person's ego to the larger reality called God or Self.

To say that there is nothing good or bad but thinking makes it so is to look at the matter only from the standpoint of the ego. If there is only a relative point of view about evil, the egocentric person may justify any actions to his own satisfaction, evaluating them in terms of whether or not they suit his own egocentric ambitions, desires, and wishes. Great deviltry can be justified in this way. But if there is another point of view about what is evil, from the Divine Viewpoint of the Self or God, then this relativism of the ego can be shown up for what it is: another example of human egocentricity.

Is there a viewpoint about evil that is different from that of the ego? The story of Moses and the guiding angel, Khidr, found in the 18th Sura of the Koran, suggests that there is.

In this tale Moses and Khidr are traveling together when they come to a village and Khidr unaccountably sinks all the boats. Moses is shocked at what he regards as an evil, but later he learns that robbers would have stolen the boats, and that Khidr, by sinking them, actually thereby saved them for the villagers. Next Khidr falls upon a young man and kills him, which apparent evil act shocks Moses again, but soon he learns that the young man was about to kill his parents and it was better for him to die this way rather than to become his parents' murderer. Finally Khidr makes a wall collapse, much to Moses' dismay, only later it appears that this discloses a treasure for two orphans. Because Moses persists in being shocked at what Khidr does, and consistently fails to perceive the hidden goodness in his acts, Khidr is forced to leave him.

In this tale Moses views events from the limited viewpoint of the ego; Khidr has the larger viewpoint of the Self. Moses' standpoint is not exactly egocentric, and we are sympathetic with his strong feeling reactions of horror at the things that Khidr does, but nevertheless his standpoint is limited by the narrow range of ego consciousness. Khidr does not have that limitation but sees the total situation in much broader terms. He has, so to speak, the advantage of a Divine Perspective.

In much the same way many people discover in the process of psychotherapy or their spiritual growth that what they originally thought was an evil event was really something quite positive. Many persons, for instance, frightened and overwhelmed at some breakdown in their lives, are forced to undergo powerful transformations in their personality which they later realize were good. They then view the original dark condition as a blessing since it drove them to make the creative changes. In fact, I think it can be said that no true healing ever occurs unless a person does begin to see good and evil in his or her life from the broader viewpoint of the Self, instead of from the limited viewpoint of the ego. It is not too much to say that the healing of the soul is, fundamentally, a reevaluation of good and evil, and therefore a shift from ego to Self.

So far I have suggested that what is good and what is evil can be decided from any one of three standpoints: (1) The egocentric standpoint, that is, whether or not events support or are against our egocentric goals, ambitions, and desires. The standpoint of the Puritan divines, for instance, can be said to have been egocentric; since the epidemic suited their purposes, they decided it was good and part of God's plan. (Whenever we enlist "God" and place Him in the service of our egocentricity there is hell to pay.) (2) The second standpoint that may determine for us what is good and what is evil comes from human feeling. We saw this in the case of the story of Moses and Khidr in which Moses had strong feeling reactions against the things that Khidr was doing, although when he saw things as Khidr saw them, his same feeling function evaluated Khidr's actions differently and concluded that they were good after all. (3) The third standpoint which may determine what is good and what is evil could be said to be the Divine Standpoint. Looked at in this way what may appear to be good or evil, from the point of view of our human ego, may not be so; we cannot be certain until we think from the larger viewpoint of the Self or, to use religious language, of God.

The feeling function as a means of determining good and evil is so important a contribution of psychology to the problem that it deserves more elaboration. If, as you read of the Puritan divines rejoicing in the suffering and death of the Indians, you had a reaction of repugnance and, perhaps, said to yourself, "How terrible!" then this was a feeling reaction and is an example of what Jung called the "feeling function." As C. G. Jung has shown, people are oriented in life by one or more of four psychological functions, which he calls thinking and feeling, sensation and intuition. It is the feeling function that impels us to make statements of *value*. It can therefore be called the "valuing function." A person with a well–developed feeling function reacts to something as good or bad, beautiful or terrible, just or unjust. People with little or no feeling do not react to situations with an appropriately human value judgment; because they don't they are more likely to become the instruments of evil. Without some development of feeling a person will scarcely be human and is much more likely to have an exclusively egocentric viewpoint about what is evil.[5]

The feeling function is generally devalued in the Western world today, which is unfortunate because it is essential in the struggle against moral evil. If, for instance, you study the events that took place in Nazi Germany you may cry out, "What? No feeling response? Was there no voice anywhere crying out against these horrors?" Yet similar examples of atrocities against people, with no feeling response to mitigate the evil, can be seen in other countries of the world too.

On the other hand, we can also say that evil in the world *develops* the feeling function. If it were not for the existence of evil, there would be no feeling reactions. So the matter is paradoxical, and we get a hint here of what we will look at more closely as we progress further into this study: that evil may be necessary if we are to become complete human beings. For if a complete human being is a feeling being, then evil must be allowed to exist for this feeling nature of ours to live and grow.

But even the feeling function, as we saw in our story of Moses and Khidr, may be mistaken, for it too is limited by the narrow range of ego consciousness. For this reason mankind has always longed for the standpoint of the Self, that is, has hungered to see reality as God sees it. And religion has obliged by offering to mankind its Ten Commandments, its codes of supposedly divinely sanctioned morality and its metaphysical overview of life which, because it transcends the ego standpoint, offers the hope of a greater view of good and evil.

Psychology also, although much more humbly, offers the ego the opportunity to acquire a larger view of good and evil by encouraging a relationship with the Self. One way this is done is through the study of one's dreams, for dreams can be shown by psychology to express the standpoint, not of the ego, but of the Self. To be in contact with one's dreams, therefore, is to have the hope of altering one's ego standpoint in the light of a larger reality.

Perhaps two illustrations will give us an idea of how this can occur. In my book *Healing and Wholeness*,[6] I summarized the case of a young Nazi aviator who came into Jungian analysis during World War II in Berlin because he suffered from hysterical color blindness, and so was incapacitated for his military duties, for which reason his military superiors sent him to the analyst for treatment. This young aviator was totally identified, on a conscious level, with Hitler, the Hitler Youth Movement, and the goals of the Third Reich. The analyst asked for dreams, and finally some dreams came. But the dreams, as the young aviator said, turned everything upside down, and were "just the opposite of life." For in his dreams Hitler appeared as an evil man with his hands dripping with blood, while a hated sister, who had joined the underground, appeared as a holy person whose face was shining white. Shocked at his dreams, the young aviator decided to investigate matters for himself and went to visit a concentration camp. What he saw here opened his eyes and appalled him. He wrote to his analyst, "I believed too long that black was white. Now the many colors of the world won't help me any more." He then committed suicide; the revelation of good and evil was too much for him.

The story illustrates all three perspectives about evil. Originally the young aviator was identified with an egocentric view of evil. Whatever supported his egocentric desire to see Hitlerian Germany triumph was good, and whatever opposed it was evil. Then came the viewpoint of the Self, expressed through his dreams, which turned his egocentric attitude upside down. But which would win out? Many a person confronted with these two standpoints will cling tenaciously to the egocentricity, deny the viewpoint of the Self, and go on as before. But this young aviator had too much feeling. His feeling function reacted violently against the atrocities of the concentration camp and this decided the matter in favor of the viewpoint of the Self. One hopes this saved the young man's soul, even though he could not bear to go on with his physical existence under these circumstances.

A second example I have cited in my book *Dreams and Healing*.[7] It concerns a mature women who had for years been a recovered alcoholic and a member of Alcoholics Anonymous. She had learned that her sobriety depended upon her honesty with herself and other people. One day she borrowed a tape from the tape library of her Church. She decided to make a copy of the tape but in the process accidentally erased the original and also failed to make her copy. Guilt–stricken, she decided she could not face the Church's tape librarian and so simply returned the useless tape with no comment. Then she had a dream in which she was having intercourse with a certain man. When asked about the man in her dream, she said that he was a terrible man, a great con man and a liar. Immediately it became apparent to her what the dream meant: that she had given in to her own lying side and become possessed by it. With this insight she made her confession to the tape librarian. As one might expect, it was not a grave matter and the affair ended nicely.

Originally this woman acted out of her egocentricity: she could not face her guilt. But her dream presented her with the viewpoint of the Self and destroyed her rationalizations by showing her what in fact she had done: become possessed by her lying, deceptive side. Her feeling function then said, "This is terrible!" and impelled her to make her timely and healing confession.

Where might we find more knowledge of the Divine point of view with regard to good and evil, the point of view, in psychological language, of the Self? A place to start would be mythology, for mythology claims to offer mankind a broader perspective than that of the ego. It is to this that we now turn.

Notes

1 Nicholas Berdyaev, *The Destiny of Man* (New York, N.Y.: Harper Torchbook, 1960), p. 18. Underlining is mine.

2 William Brandon, *The Last Americans* (New York, N.Y.: McGraw-Hill, 1974), p. 202.

3 See Will Durant, *Our Oriental Heritage* (New York, N.Y.: Simon & Schuster, Inc., 1935), p. 734.

4 William Shakespeare, *Hamlet*, Act II, Scene 2, line 259.

5 See Marie–Louise von Franz and James Hillman, *Jung's Typology* (New York, N.Y.: Spring Publications, 1971), especially Hillman's article on the feeling function.

6 John A. Sanford, *Healing and Wholeness* (New York, N.Y.: Paulist Press, 1977), p. 14.

7 John A. Sanford, *Dreams and Healing* (New York, N.Y.: Paulist Press, 1978), pp. 22 and 23.

CHAPTER TWO

The Problem of Evil in Mythology

S ince human beings are forced to react to life in terms of good and evil, it is not surprising that mythologies and world religions have always tried to account for the presence of evil, each in its own way. Through their myths ancient man personified the evil forces of nature and of the spiritual world that were a threat to him and sought to come into some kind of relationship with the destructive powers that so profoundly affected his life. A review of some of the more important myths will help us see the various ways in which mankind has tried to come to terms spiritually and psychologically with the problem of evil.

C. G. Jung tells us in his autobiography of the Elgonyi, a primitive tribe with whom he lived for a while during his journeys in Africa in the 1920's. The Elgonyi, he relates, spoke of a Creator Who had made everything good and beautiful. "He was beyond good and evil. He was *m'zuri*, that is, beautiful, and everything he did was *m'zuri*." But when Jung asked them, "But what about the wicked animals who kill your cattle?" they replied, "The lion is good and beautiful." "And how about your horrible diseases?" Jung pressed them. "You lie in the sun and it is good," they replied.

Jung says he was greatly impressed by their optimism, but, "at six o'clock in the evening this optimism was suddenly over. . . . From sunset on, it was a different world—the dark world of *ayik*, of evil, danger, fear. The optimistic philosophy gave way to fear of ghosts and magical practices intended to secure protection from evil. Without any inner contradiction the optimism returned at dawn." [1]

In this way these primitive people personified the evil forces that they knew surrounded them on every side. Primitive though it sounds, this mythological outlook toward evil is more accurate than our modern materialistic and rationalistic outlook which, in denying the existence of gods and demons, and ignoring the reality of the psyche, tends to overlook the power of evil. The coincidence of much illness with psychological problems, the violent eruptions of destructive forces in war, the exploitive behaviour of man toward man, and the high incidence of crime all bear testimony to the fact that man often behaves for all the world as though he were possessed by a devil. Ancient man personified these evil powers as mythological beings or spirits. Modern psychology prefers to call them archetypes or autonomous complexes. The fact is that primitive mythology and Analytical Psychology agree that man's fate and destiny are to a surprisingly large extent controlled by autonomous psychic factors beyond his conscious control.

Depth psychology and primitive mythology thus share a common world view, because both say that in addition to outer, physical reality there is what can be called inner, spiritual reality. The one is as autonomous and objective to human consciousness as is the other. To be sure, this attitude goes against the prevailing world view of our times that denies any reality beyond that of the material world and the conscious mind. The reality of evil forces us, however, to accept a broader world view that takes into account spiritual reality as well as material reality.

Of course there is resistance to this. Modern man prefers to believe that the evils of our time somehow do not exist in the human soul or spiritual sphere, but have political or economic causes, and could be eliminated by a different political system, more education, the correct psychological conditioning, or one more war to wipe out the enemy, for he does not want to see that the enemy is to be found in the devils and demons in himself.

Morton T. Kelsey, in his fine book *Myth, History and Faith*, has this to say about our reluctance to look at the origins of evil and the reality of a destructive principle: "First of all, secular man in this century has been brainwashed by materialistic thought. In a rational and materialistic world there is no place for such a principle of destructiveness. It is neither rational nor material, and so it cannot exist. If one is to consider the possibility that evil is something more substantial than just the absence of good, then he has to overhaul his whole world view, and this is a very painful and difficult task. It is better simply to deny the reality of any such principle out of hand." [2]

As mankind became more developed, mythology also became more sophisticated, and gradually there emerged a distinct pantheon of gods and goddesses, one of whom was sometimes said to be the author of evil. Some of these mythologies seem to anticipate the later Christian idea of the devil.

For instance, among the Egyptians, we have the evil god, Set, who is contrasted with his good brother, Osiris. Osiris makes the earth fertile, brings the life–giving water, and sheds light upon the world. Everything that is a blessing to human life, everything beneficent and creative, comes from him. Set is his eternal adversary, a personification of the arid desert, the bringer of darkness and drought. From him comes everything destructive and inimical to human life.

The good Osiris falls victim to a plot by his evil brother, Set, who builds a beautiful chest just the right size for Osiris, invites him to a great feast, and offers the chest to whomever it will fit. Unsuspecting, Osiris enters the box and Set and his accomplices rush upon it, nail it shut, and cast the chest into the sea. Isis, Osiris' mother–wife, eventually finds the body of her son–lover and rescues it, but Set happens upon Osiris' remains, and to ensure his eternal destruction he divides his brother's body into fourteen pieces and scatters them about the earth. However, Isis recovers Osiris' dismembered body, except for the phallus, which had been greedily devoured by the great crab, Oxyrhynchid, who was forever cursed for this dark deed.

After this Osiris cannot return to rule the world of the living again, but he rules the Underworld, where he is the judge of the dead. His place among the living is now taken by his son, Horus, who, upon reaching maturity, resumes the struggle against Set and spreads the blessings upon mankind that Osiris once shed.

Among the Norse, the god Loki personified evil, in contrast to the beautiful and much beloved Baldur. Baldur was so beautiful that he shed light wherever he went; none could equal him in wisdom, and merely to see him was to love him. He was the favorite of gods and men alike. But Loki was a mischievous, malevolent deity who loathed Baldur and plotted his downfall. It seemed that every living thing had taken a pledge not to harm the beautiful Baldur except the mistletoe plant, which had been over-looked. Loki proceeds to make a shaft of the mistletoe plant, and joins the other gods who are having a game in which they hurl things at Baldur, confident that nothing will hurt him. Loki per-suades the blind Hod to take the mistletoe and fling it at Baldur, which he does trustingly, but lo! the mistletoe pierces the beauti-ful god who sinks dying to the ground.

The split between a good god and an evil god is greatest, how-ever, in the Iranian (Persian) myth of Ahura–Mazda and Ahri-man. From Ahura–Mazda came life, light, truth, and the bless-ings of mankind. From Ahriman came death, darkness, lies, and the ills of mankind. The world in which men live was the battle-ground of these two gods, and human souls were their prize. Ahriman does not fight alone. He is the prince of demons, and commands a host of Daevas, evil beings devoted to trickery and falsehood, who strive, along with their master, to destroy the power of good that Ahura–Mazda represents, and to draw man-kind into evil ways. Never before or since have the opposites of good and evil, light and dark, been as sharply drawn as in the Iranian religion, for while Set and Osiris, Loki and Baldur, are gods in conflict with each other, they are still but two among many deities, while Ahura–Mazda and Ahriman are the chief deities of the Iranian pantheon, each the leader of one half of the spiritual realm. Nevertheless, Iranian mythology is more op-timistic than that of the Norse, for while in Norse thought the world of the gods and man crashes to a gloomy end in the apocalyptic *Gotterdammerung*, or "Twilight of the Gods," in Per-sian mythology it is said that eventually Ahura–Mazda will have the better of the cosmic duel. That this Iranian mythology influ-enced Christianity is evidenced in one of the names in the New Testament for the devil: Beelzebub, which means "lord of the flies," and comes from the lore about Ahriman, who was said to have entered the world in the form of a fly.

Zoroastrianism reappeared much later in Manichaeism, which originated with Mani, born in Persia in about the year 215 A.D. Mani taught that light and darkness, good and evil, creation and destruction, are in eternal conflict. Like the Gnostics, he related the world of spirit to the realm of the good, and the material world to darkness and evil. Man is imprisoned in the world of darkness and evil because he is imprisoned in his body, and salvation for man consists of separation from his body via right knowledge, plus a rejection of the passions and sexual appetites that keep him enslaved to the evil, material principle. Manichaeism was especially challenging to Christianity, partly because it resembled it so closely. It was to combat Manichaeism that St. Augustine, its chief antagonist in the fourth century A.D., reformulated the idea of evil as the *privatio boni*, or deprivation of the good, a formulation of evil we will look at more closely in our last chapter.

However, not all mythologies had the dualistic quality of Zoroastrianism. Among the Greeks, for instance, there was no single deity who personified evil. Not even Hades, ruler of the Underworld, was evil; he was no Christian devil ruling over the souls of the damned in Hell, but merely the ruler of the lower realm of the dead.

Evidently the Greeks did not need a devil because there is no god to whom is ascribed the origin of all good things; instead each deity in Greek mythology is capable of both good and evil. So the Greek gods quarrel with each other outrageously, are often petty and self–seeking, are prone to jealousy, rage, and plotting. Each of them is capable of showering blessings upon needy mankind, but, especially if their worship has been neglected, they are just as apt to be destructive. The fact is that the gods and goddesses of ancient Greece seldom care much about human life one way or the other, but they are vain enough to want their share of attention. Only Asklepius, god of healing, who was a mortal man to begin with and not one of the Olympiads, can be said to be a deity who concerned himself with the welfare of mankind, though mention must also be made of the Titan, Prometheus, whose devotion to mankind led him to steal fire from heaven and suffer a cruel punishment from Zeus as a consequence. But these are rare exceptions among a pantheon of deities singularly undistinguished in their overall concern for human welfare. With such a pantheon of gods and goddesses, each of whom is sometimes good and sometimes bad as far as human beings are concerned, there is no need for a devil who personifies the evil principle.

American Indian mythology is unique in that it embodies both monotheistic and polytheistic elements. There was an almost universal belief among the Indians of what is now the United States in a Great Spirit whose power and authority were supreme over all life. Lesser deities, mankind, and all of nature were under the ultimate rule of the Great Spirit who was beneficent and just. However, the qualities of the Great Spirit were only vaguely defined, and while he was beneficent, he also left the actual running of the created world largely up to a variety of lesser spirits of a theriomorphic nature.

These lesser spirits were spirit powers who directed the actual workings of the universe and nature, and man must constantly ask for their help and guidance. From contact with one or more of these autonomous spirits, a man or woman might gain "medicine" for his or her life. For the most part they were beneficent powers, but some of them were responsible for evil as well. The Indians believed man lived in a world of constructive and destructive forces, a world of elements that were helpful to man but also were inimical to him. Nature, the Indians knew, showered her blessings upon needy mankind, but could also be cruel.

Sometimes the evil power in Indian mythology was simply a personification or abstraction of the destructive side of nature. Among the Iroquois, for instance, there was the recognition of a perpetual struggle between the god of life, who caused nature to be warm, fertile, and bountiful, and "Stony Coat," the god of ice and winter, whose function was to destroy. But Stony Coat was not an Ahriman, seeking to destroy the moral fibre of man's soul, and pitted in a desperate struggle to win power over all the universe; rather he seemed to be simply the dark, unrelenting, and cruel side of nature. Stony Coat was the Iroquois way of personifying their belief that life was a constant struggle between light and darkness, good fortune and bad.

However, the Indians sometimes did assign the origin of good things to certain spiritual beings and evil things to another, so they frequently told myths of the two brother gods who each embodied one side of life. Among the Algonquins, for instance, the hero god Gluskap had his evil wolf–brother Malsum. It was Gluskap who made the pleasant places to live, the good food and beneficent animals, and the human race, while Malsum made rocks, thickets, swamps, and poisonous and unpleasant animals. Malsum also tried treacherously to kill Gluskap by finding out the only plant (also the mistletoe) that was able to harm his good brother, in a manner reminiscent of the Norse story of Loki and Baldur, and the Egyptian tale of Set and Osiris. But the Indians were usually optimistic in their final outlook. In this particular tale, Gluskap eventually succeeds in escaping from Malsum's evil plots and overcoming him.

A widespread Indian story told in various versions involved an evil ghost who had no body but a rolling head. In the Natchez Indian version, the story begins with two brothers, one of whom dies, but his head lives on and begins to persecute the surviving brother and his wife. After many adventures and narrow escapes, the one brother finally succeeds in evading the ghostlike rolling head of his deceased sibling and undoing his power.

Among the woodland Indians of the East, a favorite tale of good and evil involved the twins Taweskare and Tsentsa. The former insisted on emerging from his mother by kicking his way out of her body and in doing so killed her. Thus his beginning was destructive, even though his brother remonstrated with him and urged him to be born in the usual way. The good brother, Tsentsa, proceeded to go about his business of creating the world, but when he was resting, the evil Taweskare would undo all the work his brother had done. So when Tsentsa made the fertile plains, Taweskare made the harsh and forbidding mountains and the jagged, inhospitable canyons and lonely swamps. It was Tsentsa who made trees and bushes with good fruit, but Taweskare who put the thorns on many plants.

Among the Pawnees the good power was represented by the North or Morning Star, who assisted the sun to rise each day into the sky. The evil power was represented by the South or Evening Star, who dragged the sun down into the underworld each night. Morning Star was a protector of mankind, but Evening Star was a dangerous enemy. However, the ultimate conclusion was optimistic, for in the end Evening Star died and where he had been pierced by magic arrows he gave great blessings to mankind.

In such stories the Indians tried to account for the obvious evil in the world. However, there was no single figure who opposed the Great Spirit, and no devil who deliberately tried to distort and win men's souls. The closest figure to a genuine devil would be the figure of Trickster, a fascinating character in Indian tales and legends over most of the continent of North America. Variously called Coyote, Saynday, Old Man, Raven, Spider, Wisagatchak, Rabbit or Wakdjunkaga, Trickster is a morally inferior being with ludicrous qualities. In many tales, for instance, he is represented as having a gigantic penis, which he must sling over his shoulder as he travels along. Moreover, he can detach this penis from himself, and with this trick he engages in many sexual exploits and adventures of the sort usually forbidden to Indian men. Trickster has little conscience, but great mischievous power. He, more than anyone else, is responsible for the fact that the creation does not operate in a smooth manner; he is, as it were, constantly throwing a monkey wrench into the otherwise good creation fashioned by the Great Spirit. However, he does this more by bumbling and foolishness than any deliberate malevolent intentions, and is certainly not capable of any concerted effort to overcome the Great Spirit as the Christian devil is able to do against God. Moreover, sometimes Trickster actually brings about a better state of affairs after his foolish actions, and occasionally, as in the Nez Perce creation story "Coyote and Monster," is actually a heroic figure benefiting mankind. In addition, he is usually a figure more fooled himself than fooling others (as Shakespeare put it, more sinned against than sinning), and a figure who is laughable if not lovable.

There is, then, no deity in American Indian mythology who corresponds to the devil of Christianity and Zoroastrianism, and most Indians were perplexed at the Christian idea of a satanic being. They accepted it as a fact that human beings combined in themselves both good and evil, and did not need to invoke the idea of a devil to explain why some people had a bad heart and some a good heart. To represent the dual nature of mankind they often painted their faces white on one side and black on the other for religious ceremonial purposes.

The lack of emphasis on a deity who embodied moral evil may

also stem from the fact that Indian culture was primarily a shame culture rather than a sin culture. That is, life was regulated not by the idea of a deity who lays down rules for man and teaches him about sin, but by the fact that certain types of behaviour would bring shame and ostracism upon a person from the other members of the tribe. And since existence within the tribe was essential for survival, this sense of shame provided a powerful force to regulate human behaviour. The system worked quite well, and the Indians were devoid of anything like the police force, complex laws, courts of justice, jails, and psychiatric hospitals we require in order to try to regulate our behaviour.

Nevertheless, there was a strong sense of right and wrong among most American Indians. The path of evil was to be avoided, the wise men among them emphasized. Indeed, to keep the human soul from falling into evil and wandering from the true path, the Great Spirit sent mankind dreams, which should be heeded carefully. In this way the Indian could look to a source of guidance for right conduct in his life which could lead him beyond his egocentric aspirations. And the problem of evil did weigh heavily upon sensitive Indian spirits. So Chief Joseph said, when many of the exiled Nez Perce Indians were dying on the reservations in Indian Territory after their unsuccessful fight for freedom in 1877: "We buried them in this strange land. The Great Spirit who rules above seemed to be looking some other way, and did not see what was being done to my people." [3]

The point of view about evil expressed in much American Indian mythology can be said to lie roughly in between evil as exemplified in the dualistic mythologies of the Norse, Egyptians, and Persians, and the synthesized mythology of the Greeks. For in American Indian thought, while there is no specific representation of an evil deity opposing the Great Spirit analogous to Ahriman, who opposes Ahura–Mazda, there are many myths dealing with lesser spirits who are definitely malevolent in intentions, and who balance out the spirits who are helpful to man. But in all of these myths we can see two messages. First, the message that there is an autonomous power of evil that is beyond man's control. Second, the message that there is a balance of opposites in life: that light must be opposed by darkness, and that the more the light, positive side is stressed and personified in the figure of a beneficent diety, the more inevitable it becomes that the dark side will likewise appear in a god or goddess who is as evil and malevolent as the light deity is good and well intentioned.

Psychology points to similar findings, which is not surprising since mythology is a kind of map of the human psyche, a personification of the archetypal and eternal psychic forces that make up mankind's inner universe. As we will explore further in this study, there is an inevitable dark side to our nature that refuses to be assimilated into our lofty ideals of goodness, morality, and ideal human behaviour. Indeed, if we strive to be too good we only engender the opposite reaction in the unconscious. If we try to live too much in the light, a corresponding amount of darkness accumulates within. If we go beyond the bounds of our natural capacity for love and kindness, we build up an opposing amount of anger and cruelty within us. Psychology warns us against trying to be better than we are, and urges us to strive not so much for a forced "goodness" but for consciousness, and to live, not out of ideals we cannot keep, but from an inner Center which alone can keep the balance. The grounds for the moral life are thus shifted from a striving for the highest moral ideals (though moral ideals are also important) to a striving for self-knowledge, in the belief that man's moral values and ideals are only effective within the scope of his consciousness. To try to be good, and disregard one's darkness, is to fall victim to the evil in ourselves whose existence we have denied.

In mythological language, we cannot honor a beneficent deity of light and love, and disregard his dark and sinister brother. For it is precisely when Ahura–Mazda tries to establish his hegemony over the world that Ahriman wars against him. It is exactly at the moment that the gods try to make the beautiful Baldur invulnerable that Loki succeeds in his plot to destroy him. It is precisely when Isis favors Osiris and despises Set that Set is able to bring about Osiris' downfall. Only among the Greeks was there no war among the gods (quarrels, maybe, but not wars), for these gods and goddesses were too wise to claim to be good. So psychology suggests that we reject any pretence of being good that forces us to keep our evil hidden from ourselves. We thus follow the example of Jesus who, when he was addressed by the rich young man as "Good Master" retorted, "Why do you call me good? No one is good but God alone." [4]

Notes

[1] C. G. Jung, *Memories, Dreams, Reflections* (New York, N.Y.: Pantheon Books, 1961), p. 267ff.

[2] Morton T. Kelsey, *Myth, History and Faith* (New York, N.Y.: Paulist Press, 1974), p. 35.

[3] *The Great Chiefs* (Alexandria, Va.: Time-Life Books, Inc., 3rd ed., 1975), p. 183.

[4] Mark 10:17–18.

CHAPTER THREE

The Problem of Evil in the Old Testament

O ur résumé of some of the most important mythologies of good and evil gives us an idea how the human
mind has always grappled with the problem and tried
to come to terms with it. We have seen how the figure of a god of
pure evil appears in those religious outlooks that accentuate
goodness and personify its origin in a distinct divine figure. However, as Westerners, our psychology and outlook are inevitably
shaped by the Judaeo–Christian tradition, which is so regardless
of whether or not we believe in the tenets of these faiths. Because
of this tradition, the main focus of this book will be on Judaeo–
Christian ideas relating to good and evil and their relationship to
psychology. So now we will study the devil and evil in the Bible,
starting with the Old Testament.

In the Old Testament there are only four references to Satan as
a supernatural being, and all four of these are found in the post–
exilic books (later than 597 B.C.). Furthermore, none of these references is very important in the Old Testament narrative.

In Zechariah 3:11ff we are told that Joshua, the high priest,
appears with the angel of God, who stands on one side of him to
defend him, and Satan, who stands on the other side as an accuser. Here Satan personifies an evil being who seeks to destroy
Joshua's soul and opposes the angel who acts in Joshua's defense.
Yet this Satan has no autonomous power to destroy Joshua on his
own; he can only accuse him before God, hoping that God will
execute the sentence.

A second Satan passage is found in 1 Chronicles 21:1, which
retells the story we find originally in 2 Samuel 24 of how David

took a census of the people of Israel. In the original version we are told that David decided to number the people of Israel, which was a sin because Yahweh had forbade any such counting of heads (perhaps because of an ancient belief that if you counted anything it laid those beings open to evil spirits). However, in the Chronicles version we are told that it was Satan who "stood up against Israel, and provoked David to number Israel." So here we read of an evil power that works upon man to influence him to break the law of God in order to fulfill a destructive purpose.

A third Satan passage is found in Psalm 109:6 (King James Version), a verse of no great interest except that it refers to Satan in his characteristic role of an accuser. We read, "Set thou a wicked man over him: and let Satan stand at his right hand."

Finally, we have the references to Satan in the Book of Job, clearly the most interesting of these Old Testament passages. Here we see an interim stage in the separation of God's dark side from Himself and its personification as a separate being opposed to God. For in the Book of Job Satan is represented as one of the sons of God dwelling in God's court with Him. Here Satan seems to be a part of God's inner family and not yet a definite adversary to God's purposes; yet he is personified as different from God Himself and is able to talk with God as a separate being. It is because of the dialogue between God and Satan that the misfortunes come upon Job, for Satan accuses Job of being faithless to God, and says that Job would renounce God if God did not shower him with so many blessings. It is to prove Satan is wrong that God allows him to send misfortunes upon Job. We can take Satan in the Book of Job, therefore, as a kind of dark, doubting thought in God Himself which succeeds in producing a good deal of mischief.

Now the reason for the paucity of references to Satan in the Old Testament is that in the Old Testament it was Yahweh Himself Who was responsible for evil, so the figure of a devil was not necessary. There are many examples in the Old Testament that show that the ancient Hebrews believed Yahweh to be the originator of evil as well as good. For example, consider Amos 3:6: (KJV): ". . . . Shall there be evil in a city, and the Lord hath not done it?" Or Isaiah 45:5–7: (KJV): "I am the Lord, and there is none else . . . I form the light, and create darkness: I make peace, and create evil; I the Lord do all these things." Or Isaiah 54:16: "I create the blacksmith, who builds a fire and forges weapons. I also create the soldier, who uses the weapons to kill." [1]

Another striking example of Yahweh as the originator of evil is found in 1 Samuel 18:10. Having been rejected by Yahweh, whose prophet Samuel has pronounced a sentence of doom upon him, King Saul falls into periodic depressions. His councilors send for a skilled musician to cure him of his dark moods, and this turns out to be David. As Saul's paranoid state deepens and his fears increase, his black moods become increasingly obsessive, and he has dark fantasies about David himself, even though it is David's music that offers him temporary relief. Finally one day, as David plays for Saul, the king seizes a spear and hurls it at him. The Bible at this point says, ". . . an evil spirit from God seized on Saul." In the New Testament, as we shall see, such a dark mood and violent rage would be attributed to an evil spirit from Satan, while in the Old Testament story of Saul it is said to be from God.

Because Yahweh is a totality of opposites, everything comes from Him, including good and evil. So for the ancient Hebrew there was no problem of evil. There was only one God for them, and if there was good and evil in the world, if man suffered tragedy as well as received blessings, if human beings succumbed to dark moods and evil passions, all these things must originate with Yahweh. Not until the Hebrews' moral consciousness began to develop further did they begin to be uncomfortable with the idea of a God who apparently indiscriminately sent both good and evil upon mankind.

It would be easy to dismiss the Old Testament image of God as primitive, something interesting perhaps from the point of view of the development of the idea of God, but not something we need take seriously any longer. Yet, for all of its primitive quality there is a basic integrity to the image of God that we find in pre-exilic biblical literature. We may be bothered by the idea that Yahweh sends good as well as evil, but it nevertheless presents us with a bold and unflinching monotheism. The ancient Hebrews, with their instinctive religious genius, were grasping the idea that there was one underlying reality to all phenomena, and if this meant that evil, as well as good, came from Yahweh, then this was a conclusion to be faced fearlessly.

No less a religious philosopher than Aurobindo felt much the same way as the ancient Hebrews. In a brave statement about the nature of evil Aurobindo said:

> We must look existence in the face if our aim is to arrive at a right solution whatever that solution may be. And to look existence in the face is to look God in the face; for the two cannot be separated . . . This world of our battle and labour is a fierce dangerous destructive devouring world in which life exists precariously and the soul and body of man move among enormous perils, a world in which by every step forward, whether we will it or no, something is crushed and broken, in which every breath of life is a breath too of death. To put away the responsibility for all that seems to us evil or terrible on the shoulders of a semi-omnipotent Devil, or to put it aside as a part of Nature, making an unbridgeable opposition between world–nature and God–nature, as if Nature were independent of God, or to throw the responsibility on man and his sins, as if he had a preponderant voice in the making of this world or could create anything against the will of God, are clumsily comfortable devices . . . We have to look courageously in the face of the reality and see that it is God and none else who has made this world in His being and that so He has made it . . . The discords of the world are God's discords and it is only by accepting and proceeding through them that we can arrive at the greater concords of his supreme harmony, the summits and thrilled vastnesses of his transcendent and his cosmic Ananda (Divine Joy).[2]

However, as Rivkah Scharf–Kluger points out in her excellent book, *Satan in the Old Testament*,[3] there is a worldly, ordinary use of the word Satan that is most instructive for our purposes. For while the word Satan is only used four times to refer to a divine being responsible for evil, the word is used in other places in the Old Testament with its original meaning of an adversary. In these cases the word does not refer to a divine being, but is used in a secular way. For instance, in 1 Samuel 29:4, David fled to the Philistines for sanctuary from the enraged Saul. The Philistines are now planning to march to battle against the Israelites and do not want David with them "lest in the battle he be an adversary (satan) to us." And in 1 Kings 11:14 and 23 we read that "the Lord stirred up an adversary (satan) unto Solomon, Hadad the Edomite . . . and God stirred him up another adversary (satan), Rezon, the son of Eliadah . . . and he was an adversary (satan) to Israel all the days of Solomon."

According to Dr. Scharf–Kluger, the word satan means literally, in its verbal form, "persecution by hindering free forward movement." As a noun it means "an adversary" or "an accuser." As such, the word found frequent use in ordinary language. Indeed, Yahweh Himself could prove to be an adversary (satan) to man, as is seen in the story of Balaam which we find in Numbers 22.[4]

Balak, king of Moab, is alarmed because the Israelities are approaching his country from the Sinai desert. So Balak sends for the prophet Balaam, hoping that Balaam will pronounce a curse upon the Hebrews. "For this I know," Balak says of Balaam, "the man you bless is blessed, the man you curse is accursed." After some hesitation, Balaam consents to go to the land of Moab, so he saddles his she–donkey and off he goes. Now this made Yahweh angry, and so Yahweh sent his *malak Yahweh* (his messenger, agent, or angel) to bar the way. The donkey sees the *malak Yahweh* standing in the way, turns off the road, and runs away into the open country. This makes Balaam angry. He beats his donkey and drives her back onto the road, but they have not gone far before the donkey once again sees the angel. They are now on a narrow part of the path with cliffs on either side; the frightened donkey brushes Balaam against the cliff, and Balaam angrily beats her again. They go on their way once more until the donkey sees the angel standing at a spot even more narrow than the previous place, so this time she simply lies down in the road and will go no further, at which Balaam flies into a rage and beats her with a stick.

A dialogue then ensues between Balaam and the donkey as they talk the matter over, the donkey pleading that she has never let her master down and asking why he is beating her now, and Balaam expressing his frustration. Then the text says that "Yahweh opened the eyes of Balaam" so that he sees the angel standing on the road with a drawn sword in his hand. Balaam is terrified and falls on the ground prostrate on his face. And the angel says, "Why did you beat your donkey three times like that? I myself had come to bar your way; while I am here your road is blocked. The donkey saw me and turned aside from me three times. You are lucky she did turn aside, or I should have killed you by now, though I would have spared her." The finale of the story is that Balaam is allowed by the angel to proceed on his way to Balak, but only with the proviso that he will say nothing except what Yahweh tells him to say. Of course what Balaam finally pronounces is not a curse upon the people of Israel, as Balak had desired, but a declaration of the Divine Favor that they have received, and a promise of their success.

The English translation tells us, ". . . and the angel of Yahweh took his stand on the road to bar his way." The Hebrew says that Yahweh stood in Balaam's way as a *satan* unto him. Clearly, from the point of view of this story, God can become a satan to us, barring our way, and a dangerous adversary, for if it had not been for the donkey, which might personify Balaam's healthy instinctual life, the prophet would have blundered into this satan side of Yahweh and been destroyed. Nevertheless, as a result of the encounter with this dangerous, barring–the–way side of God, Balaam's consciousness is heightened. A dialogue takes place between the human will of Balaam and the Divine Will of Yahweh, and when Balaam continues on his way it is as a more conscious man than before, and a man who has set aside his personal desires in favor of a Divine Will of which he has now become aware.

The story of Balaam shows how Yahweh originally had a dark side that could be destructive to man and could operate as a kind of dark and dangerous force working against anyone foolish enough not to heed it. From such experiences came the biblical admonition, "The fear of the Lord, that is wisdom" (Job 28:28 KJV). From the point of view of psychology Yahweh in the Old Testament personified the archetype of the Self, which refers, as we saw in Chapter One, to the whole person, and to the fact that there is within us a Will greater and more purposeful than the will of our egos. To recognize the reality and power of the Self is to recognize the existence within us of something like a Divine Mind, Whose greater power and authority must be acknowledged. Insofar as the story of Balaam personifies the Self as the *malak Yahweh* who stands across Balaam's path as an adversary, it tells us that the Self has a dark, even destructive, side to it. And it is a fact that if a human being persists in going against the Self, that is, going against his or her own deepest truth, that person does run into a destructive force. So the story illustrates both the dark, daemonic side of Yahweh in the Old Testament, and also the dark side of the Self.

Here psychology corroborates the biblical images. For the Self demands from us that we become whole. If we persist in certain attitudes or directions in life that are not in accordance with this demand for wholeness, we may experience the dark side of the Self in neurotic disturbances or physical illnesses. If we do not see the power that stands in our way because we are taking the wrong direction in life, we may ultimately face destruction. Accidents, illnesses, psychoses, phobias, compulsive fantasies, all can be manifestations of the opposition that has arisen between ego consciousness on the one hand, and the demands of the Self for wholeness on the other hand. When such a psychological disturbance arises we can say that the Self has become a satan unto us, that it has adopted the stance of an adversary who may actually destroy us if we persist in the wrong course in life.

Balaam was able to avert this fate just in time because he saw the *malak Yahweh* standing in his path and succeeded in engaging him in dialogue. The conversation that ensued in the story is analogous to the dialogue that takes place between the ego and the Self when a person begins to remember and try to understand his dreams, or when he practices that technique for establishing a living relationship with the unconscious that C. G. Jung called "active imagination."[5] Dreams can be understood as proceeding from our psychic Center; they have the psychological function of expressing the Will of God for our lives. To remember them, react to them, and dialogue with them, is like entering into a conversation with the Power that has stood in our way. The result is a gradual realignment of our egos with the purposes of the Self.

Of course Balaam could have saved himself from anxiety had he paid attention to his donkey. When the donkey bolted off the path because she saw the angel in the way, though Balaam did not, it is like experiencing an instinctive reaction in our bodies, or from the unconscious, that if we listened to it, could tell us something about a wrong course we are taking in life. Minor physical flareups, disturbing dreams, mild depressions or anxieties are like the donkey in the story: expressions from our instinctive life telling us that somewhere, something is going wrong. If we pay attention to these things, we may save ourselves a lot of trouble, and be led more peacefully, and in a less frightening way, to the encounter with the Self, which the conversation between Balaam and the angel of Yahweh represents.

This is how psychology looks at such a story. It makes no difference if the story is historically true or not. Actual fact, or imaginative legend, the story embodies the same inner or psychological truth.

When we first encounter the dark side of the Self we may feel that we are confronting evil. Certainly the problem that is tormenting us—our illness, anxiety, depression, or phobia—is experienced as an evil condition, and from our human point of view it *is* an evil condition that will destroy us unless it is overcome. Most conventional Christian training today encourages us to dissociate this evil state of affairs with God. God's intentions, we are assured, are too benign to send such darkness upon us; like a well-intentioned parent, He would not visit us with such painful experiences. The biblical story of Balaam, though, is only one of many parts of the Bible which tells us that God has this dark side too, and that if we persevere in the wrong course in life we can run into the Wrath of God which will destroy us. In psychotherapy we also find that the painful state of affairs that has brought someone into the counseling situation is connected to the Self, that is, to the insistent demand from within that the suffering person become whole, and alter his or her attitudes in life to conform to the aspirations of the Self, not the ego.

For this reason we must speak of the dark side of God, and the dark side of the Self. But upon closer examination, it is apparent that the evil condition we are experiencing has the "intent" of curing us of our wrong direction in life. What is really wrong, what is really ill, is the wrong attitude we have toward life, the maldevelopment of our egos, and the symptom or illness the Self has produced is a consequence of this and can be seen as an attempt to cure us. For this reason Jung once said that we do not cure a neurosis, it cures us.

Moreover, as we have seen in the story of Balaam, there is a certain subtlety to the Old Testament understanding of the role of evil. Yahweh has His dark side, yes, a fearful side that is quite capable of falling upon man and destroying him if man persists in foolish or misguided actions. Yet, as we saw from our story, it is precisely this side of God that man may sometimes need to encounter in order to raise the level of his consciousness. This image of God as light and dark corresponds so closely to the archetype of the Self, as it presents itself in the images of the unconscious, that we cannot simply dismiss it as primitive. Rather, we must look to the ancient Hebrew image of God as a totality of light and dark, as an expression of one aspect of the truth about the relationship between good and evil.

To be sure, this leaves us with a paradoxical view of evil, and it offends our sophisticated religious sensibilities to think that under certain circumstances God might be as blindly destructive as nature herself, venging Himself upon those persons who, like Balaam, are foolish enough to blunder stupidly into His satanic side. But it is precisely this paradoxical view that is the strength of the Old Testament image of God and that could lead one scholar to conclude that Satan "proves himself to be a demonic–destructive principle firmly anchored in the plan of salvation."[6] For where would Balaam's salvation have come from had he not run into the dark and dangerous aspect of the *malak Yahweh?*

The reality of life is that the light and the dark are not always so far apart, and sometimes we do not always know where the good is and where the evil is. So Nikos Kazantzakis declares, "Someone came. Surely it was God, God . . . or was it the devil? Who can tell them apart? They exchange faces; God sometimes becomes all darkness, the devil all light, and the mind of man is left in a muddle."[7]

Notes

[1] *Good News Bible* (New York, N.Y.: Thomas Nelson Publishers, 1976).

[2] I am indebted to my friend Bea Burch for this quotation from Satprem's book, *Sri Aurobindo, or The Adventure of Consciousness* (New York, N.Y.: Harper & Row Publishers, 1970), p. 163. Originally published by Sri Aurobindo Ashram Press, Pondicherry, India, 1968.

[3] Northwestern University Press, 1967. I am indebted to Rivkah Scharf–Kluger for a great many insights into the role of evil in the Old Testament, and especially for her analysis of the story of Balaam.

[4] There are two traditions of the Balaam story, both of which are in Chapter 22 of the Book of Numbers. We are following the more ancient text beginning at verse 22.

[5] John A Sanford, *Healing and Wholeness* (New York, N.Y.: Paulist Press, 1977), pp. 140–148.

[6] Rivkah Scharf–Kluger, *Satan in the Old Testament*, trans. Hildegard Nagel (Evanston, Ill.: Northwestern University Press, 1967), p. 161, quoting Gerhard von Rad.

[7] Nikos Kazantsakis, *The Last Temptation of Christ* (New York, N.Y.: Simon & Schuster, 1960), p. 15.

CHAPTER FOUR

The Role of the Devil and Evil in the New Testament

Though we may admire the courageous and unflinching monotheism of the Old Testament, we may also have difficulty with the idea that God is the source of evil as well as the source of good. Does this mean that God *intends* evil; that He would just as soon bring about evil as good? Or that He is amoral? Naturally, then, we want to see what the New Testament has to say about the problem.

Evidently there were many people in ancient times who also had second thoughts about the Old Testament view of God as the source of good and evil equally, for when we move from the Old Testament to the Gospels we are at once struck by the prominent role of Satan, for though, as we have seen, Satan plays an insignificant role in the Old Testament, he plays a conspicuous role in the New Testament. Obviously, in the few centuries between the last books of the Old Testament and the beginning of the ministry of Jesus there was a considerable change in the thinking of the Jews about evil, for we find that in the Jewish Apocrypha, which was developed in the post–exilic era, and in many of the Jewish apocalypses which are not in the Jewish canon of the Old Testament, there emerged a highly developed demonology and angelology. Scholars speculate that the Jews may have been influenced by the Babylonians during the period of the Exile, since it is after this time that Jewish theologians interest themselves in a more dualistic view of good and evil. Whatever the reason, by the time Jesus came on the scene the Pharisees and the common people of the time were firmly convinced that there was a whole hierarchy of spirits, both good and bad, and that Satan presided over the latter.

In keeping with the important role of Satan in the New Testament, we note that he has many names. Thirty–five times in the Gospels he is referred to as Satan; thirty–seven times he is the "diabolos" or devil; many times he is called the "enemy,"[1] and seven times he is referred to as "Beelzebub," which means "lord of the flies," and refers, as we have seen, to the Persian deity, Ahriman. In the fourth Gospel we also find frequent references to the devil, where he is usually referred to as the "Prince of this world."[2]

Regarding these names, the appellations "Satan" and "diabolos" (devil) are by far the most numerous. "Satan" is a carryover from the Hebrew word that means, as we have seen, a being who hinders free, forward movement, therefore an adversary or accuser. Diabolos is a Greek word used as the equivalent of Satan. Its literal meaning in a verbal form means "to throw across"; it is as though the diabolos throws something across our path to interfere with our progress. In its noun form, diabolos is also translated as an accuser or adversary, so that it corresponds closely in meaning to the word Satan.

In the Gospels, Satan is held responsible for a multitude of human ills. He sends physical ailments and afflictions upon a suffering mankind; for instance, he is the one held responsible for the malady of a woman who for eighteen years could not stand erect, and who was said to be bound by Satan (Luke 13:16). He is also held responsible for mental afflictions, and to assist him in torturing mankind in this way Satan has a host of demons. So the many demans who possess the demoniac in the country of the Gadarenes plead with Jesus, when he casts them out, to send them into the herd of swine (Luke 8:28–34). Several of Jesus' parables deal with the activity of Satan among men, notably the Parable of the Sower (Mark 4:15) and the Tares (Matthew 13:28). But Satan is interested in citing man to rebellion against God's purposes, as well as afflicting man with suffering. So Luke tells us (22:3) that it was Satan who entered into Judas and maliciously inspired him to betray Jesus, and that Satan desired to have Peter as well (Luke 22:31).

Thus Satan, as his name indicates, appears in the Gospels as a spirit opposed to God, who throws every obstacle he can in the way of man's path to health and relationship with God, and not only maliciously brings about mankind's suffering, but also strives to turn man from God by inciting him to sin and rebellion.

Considering the prominent role the devil plays in the Gospels, it is interesting to note how little attention is given to his origin or destiny. We find no explanation in the Gospels for the presence of the devil or evil in the world, nor any statement about his ultimate end. One of the rare possible exceptions to this is Luke 10:18 (a verse we will discuss in a later chapter in more detail) in which Jesus says to the seventy–two who are returning from their mission, "I watched Satan fall like lightning from heaven." By and large, in the Gospels Satan is represented as simply going about doing his job. Apparently it seemed obvious to the people of that time that there must be such an evil being who performed his divinely assigned role in life.

This also seems to be the attitude of Jesus toward the devil and evil. Jesus certainly knows about the devil. At the beginning of his ministry, after his baptism and the descent of the Holy Spirit on him, we are told that Jesus went into the wilderness to be tempted by Satan. Only after he encountered the devil, and the evil temptations he placed in Jesus' way to persuade him to misuse his Divine Power, did Jesus undertake his ministry. Later Jesus often encountered Satan or his demonic host, especially in his healing work, and evidently agreed with the popular idea that much, if not all, illness of body and spirit was an affliction from the evil power.

Jesus seemed to regard evil as an inevitable part of creation and did not find it necessary to offer explanations for its presence in the world. For instance, in the Parable of the Tares, Jesus assumes the presence of the devil. In this parable a man sowed good seed, but an enemy came and sowed darnel among the wheat. ". . . Let them both grow till the harvest," Jesus advised in the parable, "and at harvest time I shall say to the reapers: First collect the darnel and tie it in bundles to be burnt, then gather the wheat into my barn" (Matthew 13:24–30). Even if this parable is from the early Church and not from Jesus, it seems consistent with his attitude: in this world the wheat and the darnel, the good and the evil, will both be allowed to grow. Only at the end of things will evil be separated from the good and destroyed.

Similarly, in Matthew 5:45 we read: ". . . pray for those who persecute you; in this way you will be sons of your Father in heaven, for he causes his sun to rise on bad men as well as good, and his rain to fall on honest and dishonest men alike." Here we have the image of God allowing the bad men as well as the good, the honest as well as the dishonest to live on this earth, and both receive the sun and the rain in like fashion. Hence no attempt is made by God to eliminate the presence of evil in the world.

Yet at the same time that Jesus raised no questions about the presence of evil, he made it clear that if man fell under its power it was calamitous for him. Once when Jesus felt he would be challenged by the Pharisees if he healed on the Sabbath, he declared to them, "I put it to you: is it against the law on the sabbath to do good, or to do evil; to save life, or to destroy it?" (Luke 6:10). Clearly Jesus felt man could do evil *or* do good and it *made a difference* which he did.

Perhaps the best summation of Jesus' attitude toward evil is found in Matthew 18:5–7 where Jesus speaks of the relationship of little children in the kingdom of heaven: "Anyone who welcomes a little child like this in my name welcomes me. But anyone who is an obstacle to bring down one of these little ones who have faith in me would be better drowned in the depths of the sea with a great millstone round his neck. Alas for the world that there should be such obstacles! Obstacles indeed there must be, but alas for the man who provides them!"

The word "obstacle" is, in the Greek, *skandolon,* a word that means an obstacle or stumbling block. Since the function of the devil is to throw something like an obstacle across one's path, we can see that Jesus, in referring to those who become obstacles for the little children, is talking of those who fall under the power of evil. Evil, Jesus says quite clearly, *must be* (though why it must be he does not explain), but nevertheless it is of the gravest possible consequence if an individual becomes an instrument of the evil power.

Yet although the devil is an important figure for Jesus he does not perform his ministry as part of a Divine Plan to eliminate either the devil or evil. Nor does he go to the Cross because of the machinations of the devil, but rather in order to fulfill a Divine

Plan. The teachings of Jesus, as I have tried to show in my book *The Kingdom Within*,[3] are primarily concerned with the development of consciousness and the fulfillment of the personality. We could say that in all of what Jesus taught, and in the events of the Crucifixion and Resurrection, the main emphasis is not upon evil as such but upon the development of the individual, and the relationship of the individual to God. If this is accomplished, it seems to be implied, the problem of evil will take care of itself. So we do not find in the Gospels the kind of dualistic warfare that we find, for instance, in Persian lore.

What we have instead is what might be called a kind of dualism overridden by the umbrella of a far–reaching monotheism. To put it another way, on earth it appears as though there is a dualistic system at work, with the purposes of God being thwarted, whenever possible, by the purposes of Satan. But on a larger level there is only one great Divine Plan and one God overall. From this point of view it would seem as though God *allows* evil to operate, evidently because evil plays some kind of essential role in the Divine Economy. This might be called a "monistic conception of evil."[4]

This also seems to be the point of view about evil reflected by the early Christian philosopher Origen, who taught that the whole creation was struggling for perfection, and that when, ultimately, every living creature had reached fulfillment and was part of God's eternal plan, the devil himself would be saved and evil would cease to exist. This implies that the devil and evil are allowed by God to exist for God's own purposes, and when His purposes are completed, the need for the devil having been eliminated, evil will be won over to the side of the good.

At this point Analytical Psychology makes a contribution. The deepest urge or instinct within every living creature, Jung asserts, is to fulfill itself. In human life this urge toward fulfillment does not come from our conscious minds, but from the unconscious Center of our being, the Self. Fulfillment is thus urged upon us from within. Because the fulfillment of our being requires the forging of a unified personality, in which the conscious mind and the unconscious mind are acting in unison and not in opposition to each other, Jung has called the lifelong process that aims at fulfillment "individuation," since in this process an indivisible, undivided personality is the goal.

In other words, fulfillment can only come when the conscious personality expresses in a unified life as completely as possible the totality of the personality, most of which, to begin with, is unknown to us.

For this to happen, all the various parts of us must perform their proper function, and the proper function of the ego includes becoming conscious, that is, psychologically enlightened and aware. But the ego is a sleepy bear who perfers to hibernate. Few people become conscious without *having* to become conscious, without being driven to it by necessity. And this is where evil comes in. For the most part, it is only when people encounter evil in some form—as pain, loss of meaning, or something that appears to be threatening or destructive to them—that they begin to find their way to consciousness. And only when people are tested in the fire of life, so that what is weak within them is purged away and only the strong elements remain, does individuation take place. This purging can only take place in the context of a certain amount of suffering and struggle. Paradoxically, without a power in life that seems to oppose wholeness, the achievement of wholeness would be impossible. From the point of view of psychology, then, evil is a necessity if individuation is to occur.

We can liken a person's life to a story. It is said that everyone has one novel in himself—his own life story. Yet it is virtually impossible to imagine a story without evil in it. If all the characters in a novel were always good and happy, if no tragedy ever occurred, if no dark event ever threatened anyone, if no one ever had any moral conflict, there would be no story to tell. It is evil that makes things happen, which is one reason why we are all fascinated by it and read the terrible stories in our newspapers with horrified fascination. In Goethe's great poetic drama, *Faust*, Mephistopheles complains about this. He says without him nothing would ever happen in the world, and yet people do not appreciate him! For this reason, when asked by Faust who he is, Mephistopheles replies that he is "part of that force which would do evil, yet forever works the good." [5]

Christian sages have long recognized the necessity for evil in a world which is to be morally meaningful. Can there be a just life in a world where there is no injustice? Can there be true human freedom in a world in which people are not tempted by an evil power to turn away from God? Can God raise up sons and daughters to Himself if there is no adversary who tries to make them his instead of God's? In short, can there be soul–building, the building up of consciousness, moral fibre, and strengthened personalities, without darkness, sin, and destructiveness at work in the world for souls to work against?

Of course this does not stop us from asking questions. Could not God have done it otherwise? In God's infinite knowledge and power could He not have devised another less evil world than this one that seems so grossly unfair in the way it treats many people? This is a question the Gospels do not answer. They simply imply that this is the way it is.

This point of view with regard to evil has great merit. For one thing, it is consistent with the view of evil in the Gospels and explains why Jesus did not make more of evil than he did; why he did not try to explain evil, or do away with evil. But there is also a danger in this point of view, for it can become too pat an answer, too optimistic and confident. It almost amounts to saying that evil isn't really evil, but is another form of good masquerading in disguise, since in the final analysis it promotes good. No one whose life has been truly touched by evil can accept any kind of complacent attitude toward it. Evil really *is* evil, or so at least we seem compelled to experience it. Nor does the presence of evil always guarantee individuation and the development of life. True, life might not reach its highest fulfillment without the struggle with evil, yet all too often evil wins and life is destroyed or the moral fibre of man is eroded. The accepting attitude toward evil outlined above may be correct, but if it leads us to develop a complacent attitude toward evil, it has gone wrong.

For this reason Jesus was correct in saying, "Alas for the world that there should be such obstacles! Obstacles indeed there must be, but alas for the man who provides them!" It is a timely warning that while evil may be necessary if God's spiritual plan is to be carried out and if individuation is to take place, it still remains a fact that on the human level there are experiences of evil unmitigated by the hopeful attitude that all of this is somehow necessary. Unless this is kept in mind we are in danger of slipping into a sterile, intellectual solution to the problem that avoids the deep feeling response to evil which alone gives us an appreciation of its reality.

However, this message about evil which we find in the Gospels and in Origen is not the only point of view about evil in the New Testament. For in the early Church thinking about evil soon developed a different turn which manifested itself ultimately in the teaching about the Antichrist, and this resulted in what must be called an out–and–out Dualism.

Victor Maag, in the article mentioned above, points out that the doctrine of the Antichrist is not to be found in the teachings of Jesus, nor even in the teachings of Paul. The first appearance of it, he notes, is found in Second Thessalonians (which he feels is not of Pauline authorship). The earliest Christian layer, he points out, does not seem to know anything of an Antichrist. Certainly Jesus never mentions the idea. But in Second Thessalonians we find a well–developed teaching that when the end of the world comes, a certain "son of perdition" will appear, who will oppose God here on this earth, and that this will precipitate a final, apocalyptic struggle which will ultimately result in the end of the world, the victory of Christ, and the destruction of evil. We do not yet find the term "Antichrist" in Second Thessalonians, but all the ingredients are there for the idea that flourishes in the Johannine epistles and comes to fruition in the Book of Revelation that on the Last Day Christ and an Antichrist will engage in a final struggle for supremacy.

In the Book of Revelation we have God on the one hand and Satan on the other hand. God's earthly representative in the apocalyptic struggle is Christ, and Satan's is the Antichrist. As the struggle on earth fares, so does it turn out in Heaven, so that Christ's victory over the Antichrist amounts to God's victory over Satan. And when Christ wins the victory over the Antichrist, then evil will be destroyed forever, and those who have sided with evil will share in the dreadful, eternal punishment in store for the Antichrist.

Where did this awesome teaching about evil derive from if not from the Gospels? Victory Maag traces the main ideas of the Book of Revelation and Second Thessalonians to Jewish pseudepigrapha and apocrypha. Certainly they resemble the stark dualism of the ancient Persians. But, Victor Maag notes, such a teaching is not Christian, for it does not assert that salvation has already been achieved by Christ on the Cross, but postpones salvation until a future day. The faithful are not yet saved. The Cross has not been efficacious. It all must wait for the final outcome, and though this cannot be in doubt, nevertheless salvation will not come until the end. This is one of the main reasons why Revelation was delayed entrance for so long into the canon of the New Testament, and, Maag tells us, why both Luther and Zwingli had little use for what they regarded as "... not a Christian book."[6]

What we find, then, in the New Testament, is that there is not one point of view about evil, its origin, and its place in the Divine Economy, but two points of view. The first, which we have called the "monistic view of evil" is the point of view of the Gospels and of Jesus. The second, which is an outright Dualism in which Satan and evil play no part at all in the Divine Economy, belongs to documents of the early Church such as Second Thessalonians and Revelation. Which is *the* Christian point of view? It is hard to see how any point of view about evil that we do not find in the Gospels or most ancient parts of the New Testament (such as the writings of Paul), and which deny salvation through the Cross of Christ, can be regarded as *the* Christian point of view. Nevertheless, the second teaching regarding evil has been more characteristic of the general attitude of the Church throughout the centuries than the first.

This is evident in the fate of Origen, and his idea that at the end of time the devil would also be saved. For when the Council of Constantinople in 553 rejected Origen's idea as heresy, and anathematized the most brilliant Christian thinker of the early Church, it did so on the basis of the Antichrist teaching which rejected the notion that evil could be saved or have any place at all in the overall divine scheme of things. As Maag tells us, Origen in this respect was closer to Jesus and to the Old Testament monistic attitude toward evil, while the point of view of the Council of Constantinople harks back to Zoroastrian Dualism.

Psychology has a comment at this point. The extreme Dualism of the Book of Revelation suggests a violent and unsolved split in the psychological attitude of the early Church. It is as though the psyche of the early Church was split, and this split projected itself into the metaphysical apocalyptic imagery of the teaching of the Antichrist. That such a split between good and evil existed in the minds of early Christians is evidenced in many places, but nowhere more so than in the picture Revelation gives us of those who are ultimately to be saved. For we are assured that even after Christ's final victory over the Antichrist is won, the fruits of this victory will be available to only 144,000 people. These are the only ones who have led sufficiently pure lives to merit salvation, in particular those who have had nothing to do with women. Revelation tells us:

> There in front of the throne they were singing a new hymn in the presence of the four animals and the elders, a hymn that could only be learnt by the hundred and forty-four thousand who had been redeemed from the world. These are the ones who have kept their virginity and not been defiled with women; they *follow* the Lamb wherever he goes; they have been redeemed from amongst men to be *the first-fruits for God* and for the Lamb. They never *allowed a lie to pass their lips* and no fault can be found in them.[7]

It is clear that matters have gone far beyond the picture of sin and evil given us in the Gospels. There the devil was represented as going about doing his job, tolerated by God, apparently, because it suited some ultimate Divine Purpose. But now Satan and the Antichrist are totally divorced from any relationship to any Divine Purpose. In the Gospels Jesus displays a humanitarian and tolerant attitude toward certain human frailties. He can, for instance, make the paradoxical statement to Simon the Pharisee, who was critical of the woman with a bad reputation who loved Jesus so much that she washed his feet with her tears, "It is the man who is forgiven little who shows little love."[8] But in Revelation the standard for human behaviour is so high that it is no wonder that only a small fragment of mankind will be saved. For those who are to be saved must be virgins, they must never have lied, not even once, and *no fault* is to be found upon them. Clearly, in Revelation it is man's goodness that saves him, and not the Cross, and any hint of imperfection lands man in the devil's camp forever.

If it is true, as psychology suggests, that the second attitude toward evil emerged because of a split in the Christian psyche that was not healed, then we must examine this split more closely. In the next three chapters we will look into this psychological split between what psychology calls the ego and the Shadow. But before we do, we must at least glance at the attitude of Far Eastern thought toward the problem of evil, for now we are in a position to see it in contrast to the Christian position.

*   *   *   *   *

In Hindu philosophy, good and evil are both illusions, and the opposition of good and evil vanishes in Brahman (God). As far as this earthly existence is concerned, good and evil are both necessary, or at least inevitable, but they have no place in the nature of God. Since God is not responsible for good and evil, or even concerned with good and evil (for in Hindu thought, God cannot be said to be "concerned" about anything), there is no need for a devil who is the originator of the evil principle, though there are plenty of daemonic forces that personify the evil elements in the world.

Since evil is both an illusion and a necessity as far as man's experience in this world is concerned, it is not necessary for man to struggle against evil. Salvation is achieved not by moral means, but by divorcing oneself from ego concerns, desires, and passions. This is done, not to free man from sin, but from illusion. For then illusion will die in a person, and the soul will be prepared to escape from this world and lose itself in Nirvana (union with God).

To be sure, the soul must be purified for this to occur, and this is the function of karma. The life of every being accumulates a certain karma, which is, roughly speaking, a person's "just desserts" in his many lives. The fate that is ours in life, the suffering or joy we undergo, is nothing other than the karma that we have brought upon ourselves as a result of our evil or ignorance in previous existences. This karma must be lived out; its demands must be fulfilled for the sake of the proper purging of our souls. But the fulfillment of karma, it should be noted, is not for the purpose of punishing sin, but for the purpose of cleansing the soul, and fulfilling the balance of one's life. In fact, by achieving the correct consciousness one can even set karma aside, though this is the path only the yogi can follow. The ordinary person must fulfill his karma in the correct way, hoping thereby to receive a kinder fate in his or her next existence.

Since the evil conditions of life are nothing other than karma, there is no merit in seeking to overcome evil. The sick, the suffering, the poor, are fulfilling their karma from a previous life, and nothing need be done to help them because this would be setting aside their divinely ordained fate. Man's proper task is not to oppose evil, fight against human sin, or seek to alleviate suffering, but to work to ally one's consciousness with the Will of God through renunciation of personal ego, will, and desires.

It is obvious that Hinduism's outlook on evil is different from the Christian outlook. Christianity says that God created the world good and perfect; Hinduism says that God is unconcerned with what man calls good or evil. Christianity says evil came about through an adversary to God; Hinduism says such a concept as that of the devil is totally unnecessary and is an affront to its sublime monotheism. Christianity says the root of man's problem is sin against God's laws; Hinduism says man's problem is his ignorance. Christianity says man must live the correct life and have his moral debt paid by Christ in order to be rejoined with God; Hinduism says that man saves himself by his own efforts, and that he must achieve the correct level of consciousness and divorce himself from earthly desires, and that this is the path of salvation. Christianity says God notices man, observes his soul, and judges his actions; Hinduism says that God does not notice man any more than the ocean notices the drop of rain that has fallen into its depths. Ultimately, in Hinduism, man is all but extinguished as an individual in the Godhead, much as a drop of water is extinguished in the sea. (And yet, paradoxically, does not the drop still continue to exist even in the ocean?) Christianity, on the other hand, speaks of the multitude of saints around the heavenly throne in the hereafter. It would be hard to find two more dissimilar outlooks. It is small wonder that Easterners and Westerners think so differently and have such a different psychological perspective.

One effect on Western consciousness of Hindu philosophy is the development of the idea of Reincarnation. The idea that human souls are born over and over again into this world is not drawn exclusively from Hindu thought (for instance we find it also among certain early Greek philosophers), but certainly Eastern thought is its main root. The notion of Reincarnation is in some respects a very satisfactory answer to the problem of evil, at least to the problem of injustice, for it asserts that there *is* no injustice, since everything which happens is exactly correct. If a person has a hard fate in life, that is not injustice, but represents either just desserts for sins in a previous life, or at least represents what is needed for the proper purification of the soul in this life. Thus everything that takes place is as it should be.

For this reason many people find the doctrine of Reincarnation quite satisfying and tell others how it gives them the strength to go on living this life. Many people also are able to integrate the idea of Reincarnation into their Christianity, at least to their own satisfaction, even though there is no scriptural basis for the idea.[9] On the other hand, others find the idea of Reincarnation overwhelming. "I do not ever want to have to go through this world again!" is the feeling that these people express, and for them the idea that there might be a rebirth into the world over and over again annihilates their courage.

The doctrine of Reincarnation has another difficulty: it seems an affront to human feeling. If one contemplates the horrors of Dachau and Auschwitz, the senseless death of 32,000,000 people during World War II, and similar shocking examples of what appears to be sheer evil, it seems an affront to human feeling to suggest that these victims of man's barbarity were experiencing their appropriate karma from previous lives. At any rate, the doctrine of Reincarnation is one of those ideas that is not capable of scientific exploration. There is no way to prove the reality of Reincarnation one way or the other. But what *can* be proven is that a human being can undergo the developmental process psychology calls individuation. For this to take place there must be an awareness on the part of a person of what psychology calls the shadow personality. As I have suggested, the problem of the Shadow proved to be the stone over which the early Christians stumbled, resulting in a Christian psychic split, and the attitude toward evil found in Revelation. It is to this shadow problem that we now turn.

Notes

[1] Cf. Luke 10:19 and Matt. 13:28, although these verses may well be from the early Church and not original with Jesus. See Norman Perrin, *Rediscovering the Teaching of Jesus* (New York, N.Y.: Harper and Row, 1967), pp. 112–113.

[2] Cf. John 12:31, 14:30, 16:11.

[3] John A. Sanford, *The Kingdom Within* (New York: J. B. Lippincott, 1970, and New York: Paulist Press [paperback], 1980).

[4] To borrow a term from Victor Maag in his article "The Antichrist," in the volume *Evil* (Evanston, Ill.: Northwestern University Press, 1967).

[5] Goethe, *Faust*, trans. Charles E. Passage (Indianapolis, Ind., Bobbs-Merrill Co., Inc., 1965), p. 49.

[6] Maag, "The Antichrist," p. 79.

[7] Rev. 14:3–4. Italics as printed in the Jerusalem Bible.

[8] See Luke 7:36–50.

[9] See Geddes MacGregor, *Reincarnation in Christianity* (Wheaton, Ill.: Theosophical Publishing House, 1978), for the most complete argument I'm aware of that Reincarnation is a doctrine supported by the Bible and early Church. In my view his argument is not effective, though he certainly must get a high score for trying to develop a satisfactory argument out of practically no evidence!

CHAPTER FIVE

The Shadow

The term "the Shadow," as a psychological concept, refers to the dark, feared, unwanted side of our personality. In developing a conscious personality we all seek to embody in ourselves a certain image of what we want to be like. Those qualities that could have become part of this conscious personality, but are not in accord with the person we want to be, are rejected and constitute the shadow personality.

Edward C. Whitmont states it nicely when he says, "The term *shadow* refers to that part of the personality which has been repressed for the sake of the ego ideal."[1] The "ego ideal" consists of the ideals or standards that shape the development of the ego or conscious personality. These ego ideals may come from society, parents, a peer group, or religious mores. We may consciously and deliberately select them, or they may operate more or less unconsciously to mould ego development.

Generally speaking these ideal standards of being and behaving are related in our culture to the requirements of society and to the Judaeo-Christian moral standards. So society tells us that we cannot steal, murder, or engage in other socially destructive behaviour without incurring punishment. Most of us conform more or less to this requirement and, consequently, deny and repress the thief and murderer within us. The Judaeo-Christian moral code goes further and urges us to be loving, forgiving, sexually chaste, etc. In trying to conform to this ideal we reject the part of us that gets angry, is vindictive, and has uncontrolled sexual urges.

Of course our parents are extremely important in shaping our ego ideal since they reinforce certain conduct with approval and reject other types of behaviour with disapproval or punishment.

Character–building organizations, like the Boy Scouts and similar groups with codes of conduct and standards of behaviour, also play a certain role in shaping our conscious personality.

As we develop psychologically, we come to identify with our ego ideal and reject all those qualities that contradict it. But the rejected qualities do not cease to exist simply because they have been denied direct expression. Instead they live on within us and form the secondary personality that psychology calls the Shadow.

It is as though human beings contain within themselves the whole spectrum of potential human behaviour, but some of these potentialities are excluded for the sake of the development of a specific conscious personality. Religious mores recognize the need for this, and that is why we have religiously sanctioned morality. Take the Ten Commandments, for instance. It would not be necessary to have commandments saying "thou shalt not steal," "thou shalt not commit adultery," "thou shalt not kill," unless it was likely that we might do these things. If we follow the Ten Commandments, those psychological tendencies which the Ten Commandments forbid are included in the shadow personality.

In our dreams the shadow personality appears as a figure of the same sex as ourselves whom we fear or dislike or react to as an inferior being. In fact, studying our dreams is one way to get to know our Shadow. The dream figure who represents the Shadow, or an aspect of the shadow personality, is always of the same sex as the dreamer because the Shadow personifies qualities that *could* have become part of the ego. A distinction is drawn between the Shadow, and the anima or animus, which personify the feminine qualities in a man and the masculine qualities in a woman.[2] A man, for instance, has certain feminine qualities that comprise his anima, but his Shadow embodies rejected masculine qualities that act like an alter ego. In fact, in cases of split personality, the Shadow may actually usurp the role of the ego. A well–publicized example of this can be found in the book, later a movie, *The Three Faces of Eve*. Here Eve–White is the usual ego personality, and Eve–Black corresponds to the Shadow. At times Eve–White gives way to Eve–Black, and then Eve–Black lives out *her* life. Notice that while Eve–Black knows all about Eve–White, Eve–White knows nothing about Eve–Black. This is because we are usually ignorant of our Shadow and the autonomous life it leads within us, while the Shadow, as a part of the unconscious, knows everything that goes on in consciousness.

We usually think of the Shadow in active terms, as the personification of our tendency to act in anger, or out of lust, or something similar, but the Shadow may also be a passive figure, the personification of a weakness we would rather not notice. As T. S. Eliot once put it,

> *Between the conception*
> *And the creation*
> *Between the emotion*
> *And the response*
> *Falls the Shadow.*[3]

The shadow personality can also be thought of as the unlived life. A good example of this is found in Goethe's famous poem, *Faust*. Professor Faust, 50 years old, an eminently successful scholar and renowned teacher, has reached the end of his rope. His life has dried up, his soul has become like a desert, and he even contemplates suicide. Enter Mephistopheles on the scene, and the two of them make a bargain: If Mephistopheles will do Faust's bidding in this life and see to it that Faust experiences all of the deep emotions and experiences of human life, when Faust dies he will give his soul to the devil. The bargain is sealed in blood and the story goes on to tell how Faust casts off his role as a professor and intellectual and lives out his unlived life of feeling, eros, power, and sex.

This story also points up the valuable qualities of the Shadow. For while we have largely described the shadow personality in negative terms, in fact the Shadow contains many vital qualities that can add to our life and strength if we are related to them in the correct way. In Faust's case, for instance, the unused energies of his shadow personality brought him back to life and gave him renewed vitality. We especially need the energies of our unlived lives when we reach our middle years, for at that time the energies we have been using for a long time are beginning to run out. (Of course this contact must be achieved by a psychological recognition of the shadow personality and integration of the Shadow and not through giving license to the darker side of our personality to live itself out concretely.)

But at other times, too, the shadow personality may be a boon to our personality if we can relate to it in the correct way. It may be, for instance, that a man who has tried to be kind and "Christian" in his relations with people has repressed his anger, and it now appears as part of his shadow personality. Yet if he is able to integrate some of that capacity for anger, it may help him become a stronger, more resolute person, for anger can be, as James Hillman once said, a healthy reaction to an intolerable situation. Without our Shadow, then, we may lack the capacity for a healthy reaction to life situations that are becoming intolerable to our spirit. An example of this healthy anger would be Jesus driving out the money changers in the Temple.[4] It was intolerable to Jesus' spirit that the holy Temple of God should be profaned by the people who were using it for crass commercial reasons, and so he became angry and drove them out. Obviously Jesus' capacity for controlled anger gave his personality a strength that he would not have had had he lacked the capacity for such a response.

Or, a man or woman cut off from instinctual sexual–erotic feelings may need a contact with them in order to get vital life energies they need for a healthy relationship with a member of the opposite sex.

Even the thief in us can be helpful. If, for instance, we are in touch with our own cunning thief side, we are not so likely to be taken in by other people, for our own thief–Shadow will let us in on how people dupe and cheat each other. To give an example, I once knew a man who retired from 20 years in the military service, a sincere, honest, but naive man with little experience in the tough world of business. He had a little nest egg of several thousand dollars and with this went into three business ventures within a year. In each case he was duped, not by his competitors, but by his business partners, and at the end of the year he had lost all his money. Here is a case in which it would have been to his advantage to have been in touch with his own crafty side. This would not have meant that he would have acted dishonestly, but it would have given him the necessary insight into the craftiness of other people to have protected him from their rapacity. So

Jesus says, "Be ye therefore wise as serpents, and harmless as doves." [5]

Another important help we get from the Shadow is a sense of humor. An analysis of humor shows that it is usually the shadow personality who laughs.[6] This is because humor expresses so many of our hidden, inferior, or feared emotions. For this reason another way to get at a knowledge of our Shadow is to observe what it is that strikes our sense of humor, for in our laughter we can often see our Shadow being harmlessly released.

American Indian humor may be taken as an example. The American Indians were a sexually chaste people. Sexual life was closely regulated and tribal life sufficiently confining that there was not much opportunity for men and women to digress from established codes of sexual conduct. But the Indians had a mythological character named Coyote or Trickster, whom we have already commented upon briefly, who was remarkably free of any sexual restraints. You will remember that Coyote had a very long penis and he was able to detach it from the rest of his body, which gave him the capacity for many sexual exploits. For instance, Coyote sees a number of attractive women bathing in a stream, so he hides downstream and detaches his penis which swims up the river and has hilarious sexual experiences with the women, then swims back to Coyote, who, of course, cannot be found and punished. To the Indians this story was a cause for ribald laughter as the suppressed sexual instincts in them found vicarious expression.

People in whom the Shadow is too repressed are apt to lack a sense of humor. They are also likely to be judging and unforgiving of other people, like the Pharisee who looked down on the woman with the unsavory reputation in the story in Luke 7:36–50. However, Jesus respected this woman and said that, having been forgiven a great deal in her life, she also had a great capacity for love which the Pharisee lacked because he had never made any mistakes in life, and so had never been confronted by his Shadow.

So the shadow personality is relative to the ego ideal, but there are people whose ego ideal is different from most of us. Members of a gang in the slums, for instance, may have an ego ideal that sets a high value upon aggression, brutality, and anti-social actions. In such a case the shadow personality may be light, that is,

may embody a person's more gentle, loving, and socially acceptable impulses. An example of this would be Starr Daily, a man
who deliberately set out to become a criminal. By the time he
reached his middle years he was a hardened felon who wound up
in solitary confinement. But here he had a remarkable experience
with Christ. As a result his life was turned inside out, and he lived
the rest of his days as a loving man, dedicated to the welfare of his
fellow human beings. Starr Daily tells us his story in his book
Love Can Open Prison Doors. We do not know what happened to
his former, criminal personality, but it is clear that with his experience with Christ his hitherto repressed and denied loving side
emerged. Most of us, however, try to live from our more loving,
honest, socially conforming side, and so usually when I speak of
the Shadow I will be thinking of it in its darker sense, as the one
within us who forms the dark background to our attempt to lead
a life of goodness that will meet with the approval of others and,
we suppose, of God.

It is certain that there will be the figure of the Shadow in our
personality. In order to develop a conscious personality at all we
must identify with something, and this means the inevitable ex-
clusion of its opposite. It is important that children identify with
the proper psychological attributes in the process of growing up,
and not identify with the Shadow, for if there is too great an
identification with the Shadow, the ego, so to speak, has a
"crook" in it or a fatal flaw. Individuation and wholeness are only
possible when the conscious personality has a certain moral attitude. If people are overly identified with their cheating, dishonest or violent side, and have no guilt or self-reflection, wholeness
cannot emerge.

Helping children to develop correctly in this regard, however,
is not a simple matter. Here moralistic preaching on the part of
parents, Church, society, etc., is often ineffectual or even damag-
ing. Of much more importance is the kind of life that the parents
are actually leading, and the degree of psychological honesty they
have. Moralistic preaching from hypocritical parents is worse
than useless. Of even more fundamental importance to the development of the Shadow and the eventual working out of the
problem of the Shadow is the "bonding" that must take place
between parents and children. Early in a child's life he or she

needs to be bonded by love to the mother and/or father, or to an appropriate mother or father substitute. In this way the necessary foundation is laid for a moral life, since the moral life, in the last analysis, comes down to a person's relatedness to people and a capacity for human feeling. In some children this bonding never takes place, and then the necessary emotional defenses against the darkest side of the Shadow are nonexistent or weak. This can lead to the development of criminal or sociopathic personalities, that is, to an identification of the ego with the Shadow.

But at the same time that parents encourage children to identify with their more positive characteristics, encouraging them to be honest, to have a certain regard for other people, and so forth, the parents must not split the children off too much from their dark side. For, as we shall see, the Shadow is never more dangerous than when the conscious personality has lost touch with it. Take the case of anger. Of course children cannot be allowed to give way to angry impulses in ways that are destructive to others. At the same time, it is a loss to them if they lose touch entirely with anger, since anger, as we have seen, is often a healthy response. If a parent says, "You are a bad child to be angry at your sister," there is the danger that a sensitive child may repress his or her anger in order to win the parent's approval. This results in a split in the personality and a shadow personality that is autonomous and therefore dangerous, not to mention the loss of contact with the vital energy that anger provides. This is especially destructive if the parents allow *themselves* to be angry, but not the child. "I am allowed to get angry, but you are not," is often the *de facto* attitude that parents express. So the parent has a narrow path to tread. Perhaps when the child becomes furious with his or her sister the attitude must be something like, "It is understandable that you get angry at your sister, but you cannot throw rocks at her." This encourages the child to develop the necessary restraints on the more violent instincts and affects, without cutting him off from his dark side.

Because it is inevitable that we have a shadow personality, the Shadow is called an archetype. To say something is an archetype means it is an essential building block of the personality. Or, to use the word in its adjective form, to say that something is "archetypal" means that it is "typical" for all human beings. So it is typical for all human beings that as they develop a conscious personality there will also be its dark companion, the Shadow. Because the Shadow is an archetype, it has often been represented in myths, fairy tales, and great literature. One example of the latter is Robert Louis Stevenson's novelette *Dr. Jekyll and Mr. Hyde*, a story that is so instructive we will look at it in detail later on.

It is also important that parents not punish children with rejection. Perhaps the best punishment parents can administer to children is that which is swift, and when it is over, it is over. The worst is certainly the withholding of affection and approval in order to control their behaviour. When that happens children get the message that they are bad; moreover, they are responsible for mother's or father's ill–humor, and this leads to feelings of guilt and self–rejection. To cope with such parents some children may then try desperately to conform to parent–pleasing forms of behaviour, which will result in a further splitting off of the Shadow.

If parents are to deal successfully with the shadow personality of a child, they need to accept and be in touch with their own Shadows. Parents who have difficulty accepting their own negative feelings and less than noble reactions, will find it difficult to have a creative acceptance of the child's dark side. Notice, however, that by acceptance I do not mean permissiveness. It does not help a child to have parents who are permissive toward all kinds of behaviour. There are forms of behaviour that are not acceptable in human society and children have to learn this and have to establish their capacity to control these forms of behaviour from within. In a permissive atmosphere a child's capacity to develop his or her own behaviour monitoring system is blunted. The ego development will then be too weak to enable the child as an adult to cope with the Shadow.

It can be seen that being a parent calls for unusual finesse, consciousness, patience, and wisdom if the problem of the Shadow is to be dealt with creatively. One cannot go too far in the direction of permissiveness nor in the direction of being overly strict. The key throughout is the parents' own consciousness of their Shadow problem and their capacity to accept themselves, and, at the same time, to develop their own ego strength so they can cope with their own affects. Family life in general, and being a parent in particular, is a crucible in which the shadow problem can be met and worked upon, for in family life negative feelings are certain to be constellated. For instance, at times a parent will inevitably have negative feelings toward a child—when the child misbehaves, or is annoying, or interferes with the parents' independent life, or requires too much of a sacrifice of money, time, or energy. Under the duress of family life people are certain to experience divisions within themselves. Love for a child may be contradicted by at least a momentary hatred; a sincere desire to do the best for the child may be contradicted by powerful feelings of anger or rejection. In this way we experience what divided people we are and this self–confrontation generates psychological consciousness. In this lies one great value of the shadow personality: a confrontation with the Shadow is essential for the development of self-awareness.

Because the Shadow is an archetype it is constantly reappearing in life. In fact, some persons seem fated to live out the shadow personality for the benefit of the rest of us. The criminal personality is an example. In many cases it is difficult, if not impossible, to reorient a criminally inclined personality toward more socially acceptable styles of life. In these cases it would appear that criminals are so gripped by the archetype of the Shadow that they are compelled to live out that archetype. This means that until mankind is more conscious of the Shadow, some people will be fated to live it out. In this curious way the Shadow succeeds in reaching consciousness after all, since no one can avoid the knowledge that we live in a society where some people have criminal intentions. Hopefully, a realization of this truth will soften our judgmental attitude toward others at the same time that it cures us of any tendency to be too sanguine about the potential reform of criminally inclined persons.

The question of how to deal with and relate to the Shadow is an extremely ticklish one. The Church has always known of the Shadow, even though it has not used that name, and has consistently warned us against the dark side of ourselves. Yet it has not provided an answer for the spiritual problem the Shadow poses. When we confess our sins, for instance, we are acknowledging the presence of the Shadow. Consider the General Confession on page 6 of the 1928 *Book of Common Prayer of the Episcopal Church:*

"We have erred, and strayed from thy ways like lost sheep. We have followed too much the devices and desires of our own hearts. We have offended against thy holy laws. We have left undone those things which we ought to have done; And we have done those things which we ought not to have done; And there is no health in us."

Or, in another version on page 75: "We acknowledge and bewail our manifold sins and wickedness, which we, from time to time, most grievously have committed, By thought, word and deed." Psychologically, the one in us who has offended against God's holy laws, has done those things we ought not to have done, and has failed to do what we ideally should do, is the Shadow.

St. Paul put the matter of the Shadow, and the problem it poses for Christian consciences, very clearly in the Epistle to the Romans: [7]

> I cannot understand my own behaviour. I fail to carry out the things I want to do, and I find myself doing the very things I hate. When I act against my own will, that means I have a self that acknowledges that the law is good, and so the thing behaving in that way is not myself but sin living in me . . . with the result that instead of doing the good things I want to do, I carry out the sinful things I do not want.

St. Paul has an ideal for himself but finds that something else within is thwarting his capacity to realize this ideal. His ego ideal is contradicted by some element within his own personality that causes him to act and react in ways that distress him and create in him an awareness of the need for salvation. This other one in him, which he calls sin living within him, is the Shadow. How St. Paul dealt with this Shadow side of himself is a matter we will take up in the next chapter. But it is clear that the existence of the shadow personality poses a great problem to the Judaeo–Christian conscience.

The usual way that people try to deal with the problem of the Shadow is simply to deny its existence. This is because awareness of one's Shadow brings guilt and tension and forces upon us a difficult psychological and spiritual task. On the other hand, denial of the Shadow does not solve the problem but simply makes it worse. Not only do we then lose contact with the positive aspects of this dark side of ourselves, but we will also very likely project this dark side onto other people.

Projection is an unconscious psychological mechanism that occurs whenever a part of our personality is activated that has no relationship to consciousness. This unrecognized but very much alive part of ourselves projects itself onto other people so that we see something in others that really is a part of ourselves, and this will have negative results as far as relationships are concerned. If others carry for us the projection of our own hated dark side, we will react to them accordingly. We will then hate or fear them, and will not see them as they are, with the eyes of understanding and objective discernment, but will see them in terms of our own despised Shadow. For this reason, when we encounter someone whom we hate, we do well to stop and ask ourselves if our hatred comes because something in ourselves we do not like has been projected onto the other person. This may not always be the case. Sometimes we hate or dislike other people because they are acting toward us in an objectionable way, but sometimes it *is* the case, and when it is, the relationship with that person is severely disturbed by our own unconsciousness.

This is especially likely to be the case in areas of racial prejudice. In racial prejudice we see all the people of a certain race, religious group, or ethnic minority in terms of the Shadow. Blacks then carry the shadow projection of whites, and vice versa; or Jews for Gentiles and the other way around. Naturally, this blind prejudice, based upon shadow projection, precludes the possibility of eros which always calls for relationship between individuals. An extreme case would be the Nazis, who, identified with the cult of their own superiority, projected their inferior qualities onto the Jews, with the fiendish consequences we know only too well from Buchenwald and Dachau.

Organized religion has been especially guilty when it comes to the matter of projection, for religious groups have a tendency to project their collective Shadows onto other religious groups that differ from them in matters of belief. The more rigidly persons hold to certain dogmatic religious ideas, the more inclined they are to project their Shadows onto members of other religious groups whose varying opinions would have the disagreeable effect of inculcating doubt in them. Thus Protestants have carried the Shadow for Roman Catholics, and vice versa, "Gentiles" carry the Shadow for Mormons, and Jews for Christians, while all persons who do not hold to their own fixed theological beliefs are apt to carry the Shadow for members of fundamental groups. Since people under such circumstances are totally unconscious of their Shadows and of the mechanism of projection, terrible atrocities have been committed in the name of Christ without conscious guilt about it. Christians have carried out pogroms against Jews, Roman Catholics have had their Inquisitions, and Protestants have beheaded their Roman Catholic counterparts, all in the name of the love of Christ. For when the Shadow is projected, one doesn't see the sinister intentions in oneself, the hidden enemy of doubt within, or the lower motivations of greed and self–aggrandizement that have been behind many atrocities in times past.

The above examples show that there is also the collective Shadow, as well as the individual Shadow. A group, culture, or nation has a certain collective ego ideal, which in turn creates a collective Shadow. So the Nazis, with their collective ego ideal of Aryan superiority, had a corresponding collective Shadow. The United States, with the collective ego ideal of "Manifest Destiny" (the doctrine held by the United States in the nineteenth century that it was the white man's manifest destiny to possess the North American continent), created in turn a collective Shadow that was experienced by the native American Indians, who were all but exterminated in a manner that was as ruthless and cruel as the Nazis' attempt to exterminate the Jews. Insofar as individuals within a group or nation become identical with the prevailing cultural consciousness, they too partake of the collective Shadow. It takes considerable individual consciousness to escape from such an identification, so that our individual shadow qualities, and the collective Shadow of our culture and time, inevitably become intermingled.

When we understand how an unassimilated shadow personality can be projected with such socially disturbing effects, we can begin to appreciate that this matter of the Shadow is of the gravest concern and can see how closely connected this psychological problem is to the problem of evil. For instance, war can be understood as a problem of the Shadow, which increases the importance of the shadow problem as the consequences of war today are far more frightful than they have ever been in the past. War not only gives us an opportunity to project our Shadow onto the enemy; it virtually requires us to do this, since a human being can only be brought to kill another human being when he has depersonalized that person. So the enemy must always be seen as the "huns" or "gooks" or "imperialists," never as human beings like ourselves who are fathers and mothers, sons or daughters, for then we would find it difficult to bring ourselves to kill them. Moreover, war is a socially acceptable way to let our Shadows out. In war many destructive impulses that must be denied social expression among our own people are encouraged, so that what would be regarded as psychopathology at home may be called heroism abroad. It is not too much to say that in spite of our covering over our true motives for going to war with political slogans and pious jargon, war may be brought about by the alienated, unrecognized Shadow who is yearning to express his dark nature. Many primitive peoples, like the American Indians, recognized this and required that their returning warriors undergo rites of purification before reentering the life of the village.

How a person comes to recognize his or her own Shadow is difficult to describe in general terms because it must always come about individually. We have already mentioned the fact that the Shadow lies behind most of our laughter. We have also seen that the Shadow appears in our dreams as a despised, feared, or inferior figure of the same sex as ourselves. So a study of humor and of our dream life gives us hints about the nature of our Shadow. There are also slips of the tongue, unconscious forgetting, and our fantasies.

Slips of the tongue, as Freud showed us, have an unconscious mechanism behind them, and often it is the Shadow who has produced these curious lapses in speech. For example, consider the good "Christian" woman of my acquaintance who was furiously angry with another woman but could not face it. She declared to me, "I spoke to her *venom*ently." Of course she meant to say vehemently, but it came out venomently, and venom is actually what she had in her heart toward this person, but she had been unable to recognize the fact.

Unconscious forgetting also may have its roots in the Shadow. Someone calls us on the phone and invites us to a party. We don't want to go but cannot think of an excuse so find ourselves accepting the invitation. However, the day of the party comes and goes and suddenly we realize that we forgot to attend. Why did we forget? It was a mechanism of the Shadow, the part of us that simply did not want to go, but began to plot from the first acceptance of the invitation to find a way *not* to go to the party.

So it is that if we reflect upon our slips of the tongue and unconscious forgetting, we may come across the other part of ourselves that thinks thoughts and plans actions which on a conscious level we were unable to accept.

Our fantasies also give us clues. The grocery store clerk gives us change for $20.00 when we actually gave her $10.00. Being honest, we point out her mistake and give her back her change, but, for just a moment, if we were attentive to our inner processes, there was perhaps the thought, "Oh you can keep that money and come out $10.00 to the good." Indeed, on some occasion we might do exactly that.

The Shadow expresses itself in all kinds of fantasies. For instance, our sexual fantasies may be filled with the Shadow as we fantasize having sex with all kinds of people under all kinds of circumstances, feeling guilty enough about these fantasies that we keep them carefully hidden from others and perhaps also from ourselves. For most of us immediately suppress a shadow fantasy when it occurs. Or it may be a fantasy of violence. I would surmise that there are few people who at one time or another in their lives have not had the fantasy that their husbands, wives, children, or parents were dead. With horror at ourselves we may immediately suppress such thoughts as too dark to face. Yet in fact, such shadow fantasies may simply be saying that we have not enough personal space in our lives, that our lives are too intertwined with the lives of these other people, and something in us "wants out" so more of our personal life can be lived.

Generally fantasies of the Shadow get into sex, money, and power. When there is sufficient collective support we may even give vent to these fantasies. For instance, we may allow ourselves to cheat large institutions when we would not think of defrauding individuals. There are probably very few people who have not devised various ways of going over the edge of legitimacy with regard to income tax deductions, for instance, yet they would not cheat their neighbors. I recall one acquaintance who had a car accident. He told me that he went to seven garages, got seven different bids, submitted the two *highest* ones to the insurance company (the difference between the lowest and highest bids was considerable in this case), and then simply pocketed the difference between the amount the insurance company paid him for the high bids, and the amount he actually had to pay the low-bidding garage. But I knew him to be an "honest" fellow who would never have defrauded me in such a way.

The Shadow is so strong an element when it comes to money that an elaborate system of business contracts has been devised by our society for the express purpose of keeping the Shadow out. A business contract spells out in detail what each party to the contract will do for the other and often provides sanctions in case there is a failure to perform according to the agreement. Either because one person may deliberately defraud the other, or because we find it convenient to forget what we promised when it is a matter of our own advantage, contracts have become a necessity in our culture. An American Indian would not have needed such an arrangement, for his personal word was good and was his bond, but our money-power culture has enormously exaggerated the problem of the Shadow, while the depersonalization of our way of life makes it easy for us to use other human beings as objects and not see them as individuals.

This is why the most important way to realize the nature of our Shadow is to work out our human relationships. Other people will object to our Shadow, and point out to us what we are doing to them. If we will listen to what others have to tell us, and take their objections to heart when they are valid, we will come to a recognition of our Shadow.

It is because of the dangerous situation that results from unawareness of the Shadow that psychology urges its recognition. However this recognition must be observed in the particular, not simply generalized. One may utter all kinds of general confessions, and yet totally miss a confrontation with his or her own personal dark side. We must be able to say of our Shadow what the King in Shakespeare's play *The Tempest* said of the repulsive Caliban, "This thing of darkness I acknowledge mine." [8]

It is because we must see it specifically that looking into the mirror and seeing our dark reflection meets with great resistance. Part of this resistance is perhaps the fear that if we recognize the Shadow it will overcome us; we dread seeing our dark side for fear we will become it. In practice, it is exactly the opposite way: we are much more likely to be overcome by the Shadow when we do not recognize it, for the unrecognized Shadow has myriad ways of asserting itself, as we have seen in the case of projection.

An excellent study of the Shadow, and of what happens when it is not recognized, can be found in John Knowles' novel, later a movie, *A Separate Peace*. In this story there are two friends, one of them a superior athlete who joshes and kids his friend in a kindly but irritating way that arouses his friend's resentment and jealousy. However these dark emotions are not faced, and one day the athletic friend is poised precariously on a high branch of a tree demonstrating his athletic prowess when his companion jostles—ever so slightly—the branch, causing the athlete to fall and bringing about a fatal accident. "Did I actually cause the branch to quaver?" the friend asks himself. He prefers to think he did not, and yet he knows he did. This is the way the Shadow works when it is not recognized. Had he been able to openly face his feelings of resentment and jealousy, and, better yet, had he expressed these feelings to his friend, the awful accident would not have happened. Thus over and over again we find, when we get to the bottom of things, that repression of the Shadow is not the answer.

One source of our resistance to acknowledging our Shadow is the guilt that such a realization engenders. Guilt is an uncomfortable thing to bear, and we prefer to avoid it when we can. One can observe the resistance to guilt in children, who find dozens of ways to avoid carrying the blame for situations they have caused. Many persons have not matured spiritually beyond this childish stage and simply do not want to carry the burden of guilt for the personal evil or omissions for which they are responsible. However, no one escapes the problem of guilt. Most people carry a considerable feeling of guilt most of the time, but it is a false guilt. That is, people feel guilty about the wrong things and do not carry their responsibility for the things in their lives for which they are truly responsible. False guilt cripples us, but when we shoulder the appropriate burden of responsibility for the imperfect person we are, then we are not crippled, but our personality is actually deepened and enhanced.

This also produces a considerable moral problem; rather, it brings an underlying moral problem into consciousness where we have to deal with it on a responsible level: What do we do with our Shadow? How much expression in our lives do we allow our dark side? To deny the life of the Shadow entirely, as we have pointed out, is to run the risk of having our life energies dry up. There are times when we must allow some of the unlived life within us to live if we are to get new energies for living. Moreover, if we strive to be only good and perfect, we become hateful, for too much of the vital energy within us is being denied. For this reason, there are few people more dangerous in life than those who set out to do good. It can even be said that whenever we try to exceed our capacity for natural goodness we bring about evil, not more good, because our unnatural stance generates an accumulation of darkness in the unconscious. Nevertheless, becoming a whole person does not mean giving license to the Shadow. We do not integrate our personalities if we change from being a person who is too righteous to a person who lives every impulse out without any moral or social restrictions.

The important thing, as has been said before but which must be said again for emphasis, is that we recognize the Shadow side of ourselves. This recognition alone produces a powerful and beneficial change in consciousness. For one thing, it greatly aids our humility, our sense of humor, and our capacity to be less judgmental of others. It is essential in developing a conscious personality, and therefore of individuation. It can also be said to be the basis for a truly individual morality.

As long as people observe morally scrupulous lives only because of outer sanctions, but with no knowledge of themselves, their morality is on a collective level. A higher morality can come about only through self–knowledge. Moreover, the moral values people hold are effective only within the range of consciousness. When we are unaware of our inclinations to darkness or evil, in that area of unawareness our moral codes and sense of value are ineffective, for where conditions of ignorance prevail, the Shadow remains an autonomous figure who is unrelated to the rest of the personality. For this reason, a true morality must necessarily go hand in hand with personal knowledge of one's Shadow. This is one of the great contributions that psychology has to make to the resolution of the problem of evil.

I have gone into detail with regard to the problem of the Shadow because when the matter is brought up people often ask what they are to do with their dark side. So I have tried to provide some clues to recognizing the Shadow and a few guidelines on how to live with the Shadow more consciously. However, each solution to the problem of the Shadow is an individual one, and each person must, in the last analysis, find his or her own appropriate way of living creatively with the dark side. But because the problem of the Shadow is so important, and so much a part of the problem of evil in general, we will continue to deal with it in the next two chapters.

Notes

1 Edward C. Whitmont, *The Symbolic Quest* (Princeton, N.J.: Princeton University Press, 1978 ed.), p. 160.

2 John A. Sanford, *The Invisible Partners* (New York, N.Y.: Paulist Press, 1980). See the book for a more complete explanation of how the negative animus and anima function in women and men.

3 P. W. Martin, *Experiment in Depth* (London: Routledge & Kegan Paul, 1955), p. 77.

4 Mark 11:15–17.

5 Matthew 10:16, King James Version.

6 Cf. Harvey Mindess' book *Laughter and Liberation* (New York, N.Y.: Nash Corporation, 1971).

7 Rom. 7:15–19.

8 William Shakespeare. *The Tempest*, Act 5, Sc. 1, line 275.

CHAPTER SIX

Jesus, Paul, and the Shadow

In the previous chapter I made the comment that the Church has not been too helpful to us in dealing with the Shadow. The time has come to examine the reasons for this in more detail, and I propose to do so by contrasting the attitude of Jesus with that of Paul with regard to the shadow problem.

But first it is necessary to introduce another psychological concept, that of the "persona." The word "persona" means "mask," and derives from the persona or mask worn by actors in ancient Greek and Roman drama to depict the characters they were portraying. Psychology understands the persona as the mask we wear when we go out to confront the world and other people. It is like the outer covering of our ego personality. The persona is the part of us that other people first see, and the part of us that we want them to see.

The persona has a socially and psychologically useful function. For instance, you may be feeling perfectly rotten and vulnerable on a certain day, but as you go about your various tasks and encounter other people, you cannot afford to let your vulnerability be seen by everyone. Your inner state must at times be hidden, and you need to make use of your persona in order to carry out certain functions. So an adequate persona is a necessary part of the ego's ability to cope with life and people.

Thayer Greene, Jungian analyst in New York, has pointed out in his article "Confessions of an Extrovert" (*Quadrant*, Winter 1975, Vol. 8, #2, pp. 21–32) that the persona has an even more positive role than that to play. As he has suggested, the ancient mask or persona the Greek and Roman actors wore was not used to disguise the identity of the actors, but was a means through which the actors could best express the personalities they were depicting. So the persona can also be the organ of the personality through which we express certain things about ourselves to others.

For instance, if you go to a party and carefully put on your best clothes, and adopt a gracious, charming attitude, it does not mean that you are trying to conceal your true self from others. It may be that through the persona of the clothes and the manners you can best express a certain side of yourself and best relate to people in a particular way. This is why clothing, and fashion in general, is so popular, and even necessary, for the proper clothing helps us put on the persona that is correct for a given situation.

The problem with the persona comes when we identify with it too much. When we think that we *are* that persona we are putting on, the persona is being misused. People who are identical with the persona are using it as a mask or a front. Their real personality is concealed, and they become limited to the role that the persona represents. Moreover, where there is identification with the persona, contact with the dark, shadow side of the personality is certain to be lost. So identification with a persona leads to an artificiality, a falseness, and a shallowness of personality.

Sometimes other people hand us a persona to adopt, and are uncomfortable with us if we do not assume it. A priest or minister, for instance, is almost certain to be handed the persona of being a good, kind, loving person by members of the congregation. This constitutes the role that the priest or minister is expected to assume. Other professionals, such as doctors or psychotherapists, also have personas handed to them. The psychotherapist may not be expected to be good, like the priest or minister, but is supposed to "have it all together," and the doctor is supposed to be all-knowing and incapable of mistakes. To accept a persona that other people hand us and adopt it as our own and mould our conscious personalities after it, is, of course, to lose part of ourselves. Such a persona is inevitably compensated from within, that is, somewhere in the unconscious the exact opposite of that persona is constellated within us.

Jesus would seem to have been aware of both the persona and the Shadow. For example, consider the story in Luke 18:18–19 in which a rich young man comes to Jesus with a question. "Good master," he asks, "what have I to do to inherit eternal life?" Jesus answers, "Why do you call me good? No one is good but God alone." It is clear that Jesus recognized that he was being handed the persona of being good, and he immediately handed it back.

Jesus' awareness of the persona and the spiritual dangers that come from identification with it is shown in his attitude toward the Pharisees. "Alas for you, scribes and Pharisees, you hypocrites!" Jesus says, "You who are like whitewashed tombs that look handsome on the outside, but inside are full of dead men's bones and every kind of corruption. In the same way you appear to people from the outside like good honest men, but inside you are full of hypocrisy and lawlessness." [1]

The reference to "whitewashed tombs" that look handsome on the outside is a reference to the persona that the scribes and Pharisees had adopted for themselves, while the "dead man's bones" and "every kind of corruption" is an image of the inner man or Shadow that compensates this persona identification. Jesus was quite tolerant of most human frailties, but he was indignant at this identification with the persona, and concealing of the Shadow, because it was psychologically dishonest, and led to self-righteousness, lack of compassion, and spiritual rigidity.

It is clear from these two illustrations that Jesus was aware of what we are calling the persona, and, as we will soon see, of the Shadow as well. Paul, on the other hand, had little awareness of either one. Although Paul demonstrated that he was capable of keen psychological insight into himself and his own dual nature, he did not encourage others to duplicate his spiritual efforts and wrestle with the problem of the persona and the Shadow. To the contrary, he encouraged what amounted to a repression of the problem, asking people to deny the existence of their Shadow on the one hand, and encouraging them to identify with a persona of goodness, light, and love on the other hand. So while Jesus called for a growth in psychological consciousness, and for the spiritual courage to struggle with the problem of our dual nature, Paul called for just the opposite, that is, for repression.

The passage in Romans, Chapter 7, from which I quoted in the last chapter, reveals Paul's deepest insight into himself. The extended quotation reads:

I cannot understand my own behaviour. I fail to carry out things I want to do, and I find myself doing the very things I hate. When I act against my own will, that means I have a self that acknowledges that the Law is good, and so the thing behaving in that way is not my self but sin living in me. The fact is, I know of nothing good living in me—living, that is, in my unspiritual self—for though the will to do what is good is in me, the performance is not, with the result that instead of doing the good things I want to do, I carry out the sinful things I do not want. When I act against my will, then, it is not my true self doing it, but sin which lives in me.[2]

In this passage Paul shows that he is aware of a duality in his personality; he concedes that there is another power within him that causes him to act contrary to his best intentions. We can recognize that Paul is talking of the duality between the ego ideal and the Shadow that we have been discussing. Unfortunately, Paul refuses to accept this contrary tendency as a part of himself. He declares that it is not, after all, his self that acts this way, but "sin which lives in me." This amounts to a refusal on Paul's part to accept the Shadow as an inevitable and legitimate part of his own nature; it leaves as the only possible solution an attempt to find some way to cut the Shadow off from oneself. As we have seen, this does not solve the problem, but only drives it deeper underground.

While Paul shows some awareness of the duality of his behaviour in this passage in Romans, there are other passages in which he seems curiously unaware of the significance of his words and fantasies. A glaring example is found in Galatians 5:12. Paul is warning the Galatians against the Judaizing Christians who have followed him and are urging the neophyte Christians to adopt Jewish practices, especially circumcision. Paul is angry at these Judaizing Christians who are undoing so much of his hard work and concludes his diatribe against them with the words: "Tell those who are disturbing you I would like to see the knife slip." (Literally, "I wish that those who are disturbing you might go even further and castrate themselves.")

Paul has a nasty fantasy here of his circumcising enemies accidentally castrating themselves. We can forgive him for this thought, of course, for we know what it is like to be angry, and we know the kind of thoughts that we ourselves might have under similar circumstances. What is not so forgivable is Paul's failure to see the contrast between this vindictive fantasy on the one hand and his frequent admonitions to others in the Christian community that they should never be angry but show forth and practice only love, patience, and forgiveness. Paul acts toward his Christian converts like a parent often does toward his children: anger is reserved as the prerogative of the parent, while the children are expected to be models of perfect behavior.

Paul repeatedly urges his Christian congregations to think and behave only out of what we can call their light side. Love, patience, forgiveness, gentleness, reasonableness, and lack of personal ambition are commendable and to be practiced and observed. Hatred, anger, sexual desires or fantasies, and emotions in general are to be denied. The effect of Paul's psychological ethic is the development of a collective persona. And his pressure upon his Christian converts to adopt it resulted in the repression of everything that contradicts this persona. There are many places in which Paul hands this persona to his congregations. Perhaps a few illustrations will suffice.[3]

In Galatians, right on the heels of the passage in which Paul expresses hope that his enemies will castrate themselves, he warns his Christian converts:

> . . . if you are guided by the Spirit you will be in no danger of yielding to self-indulgence, since self-indulgence is the opposite of the Spirit, the Spirit is totally against such a thing, and it is precisely because the two are so opposed that you do not always carry out your good intentions. If you are led by the Spirit, no law can touch you. When self-indulgence is at work the results are obvious: fornication, gross indecency and sexual irresponsibility; idolatry and sorcery; feuds and wrangling, jealousy, bad temper and quarrels; disagreements, factions, envy; drunkenness, orgies and similar things. I warn you now, as I warned you before: those who behave like this will not inherit the kingdom of God. What the Spirit brings is very different: love, joy, peace, patience, kindness, goodness, trustfulness, gentleness, and self-control. . . . You cannot belong to Christ Jesus unless you crucify all self-indulgent passions and desires. . . . We must never get tired of doing good. . . . While we have the chance, we must do good to all, and especially to our brothers in the faith.[4]

Obviously it would not have been necessary for Paul to admonish his converts so strongly if there had not been a powerful tendency within them, as there is within all of us, to indulge in exactly those passions that Paul decries. This part of ourselves makes up the shadow personality, and the question is, what to do with it? Paul is right that to act out all our impulses, to give complete license to our emotions and desires, can be destructive. It is not a matter of allowing ourselves to commit all kinds of lawless actions. The problem is, as we have seen, that a one–sided identification with the light side, and repression of the dark side, does not solve anything. Paul admonishes us "never get tired of doing good." He would not have to say that if it were not easy to become tired of just that. There is a part of us that refuses a one–sided identification with what Paul conceived to be goodness. An attempt to one–sidedly live up to Paul's ego ideals only reinforces and intensifies the split within us and so divides us that our Shadow becomes an enemy.

In Romans, Paul calls even more strongly for a one–sided identification with goodness: "Never repay evil with evil but let everyone see that you are interested only in the highest ideals. Do all you can to live at peace with everyone. Never try to get revenge; leave that, my friends, to God's anger." [5] There is some sound advice in this passage. It is all too likely that in opposing evil we become evil ourselves, and revenge is a dangerous motive. As an old Spanish saying puts it, "Revenge is the sweetest taste on the lips of those who are in hell." But Paul goes too far when he admonished us to be interested only in the highest ideals, and to display this to others, since this can only be accomplished by adopting a persona that belies many of our true, if unwelcome, feelings. For instance, what of that part of Paul himself that fantasied revenge on his adversaries with his crude suggestion of self–castration? By identifying ourselves only with our "highest ideals," we necessarily drive the less–than–noble parts of our nature farther from consciousness, so far that even when it blatantly expresses itself in fantasy or action, we are capable of remaining naively unaware of who we really are.

Paul is almost always antagonistic to emotion. He tends to see anger, sexual desire, and erotic yearnings as evil. Since emotions originate in the body, that is, all emotions are accompanied by measurable physiological changes, it amounts to a rejection of the physical nature of mankind. In this way Paul falls into a psychological Gnosticism. The Gnostics were a religious group in the early Christian era that rejected the material universe and man's physical self as inherently evil. In his theology Paul, and the early Church generally, repudiated Gnosticism because of its identification of the material world with evil, and held firmly to the incarnational Christian attitude that physical reality is part of God's plan. But in his ethics and psychology Paul shows that a Gnostic spirit ruled him from within: "Let your armour be the Lord Jesus Christ; forget about satisfying your bodies with all their cravings," Paul declares in the Epistle to the Romans.[6] Sex is regarded for the most part as evil; it is never considered that sexuality might be a valid expression of love and relationship. It must always be licentiousness, it must be instigated by Satan, it is never permissible except in the strict confines of marriage, and even then is a concession to human weakness while the highest way of life would be without sex entirely.[7]

Paul also handed a special persona to clergy and women. For example in 1 Timothy he says of the elder:

> ... the president must have an impeccable character. He must not have been married more than once, and he must be temperate, discreet and courteous, hospitable and a good teacher; not a heavy drinker, not hot–tempered, but kind and peaceable. He must not be a lover of money ... It is also necessary that people outside the Church should speak well of him, so that he never gets a bad reputation and falls into the devil's trap.[8]

In other words, the clergy are to live up to an extra dose of goodness. Their persona is to be such that no one outside the Church can ever criticize them. Clearly, living up to such a persona will not produce an authentic human being, but only a man who strikes a pose. Yet in practice most clergymen even today feel more or less compelled to live up to such ideals and to present such a front to people. Their congregations likewise expect such behaviour from their clergy and do not accept them should they turn out to have an ordinary amount of clay on their feet.

But the greatest difficulty with the Pauline attitude is that it is not only the deed but also the emotion and the fantasy that are regarded as evil. For Paul, to have "bad" emotions and fantasies, even though one does not act them out, is to be an evil person. So it is not just the expression of anger that is bad, but anger itself; not just a promiscuous sexual life, but sexual fantasies themselves that are from Satan.

Our fantasies and emotions, however, are uncontrollable. They are what they are and come to us from unconscious sources. Everyone, Paul included, has dark fantasies from time to time, and while we may deny that we have them, repress them, or blame them on some devilish power or other person, there is no getting rid of them. The fantasies and emotions that we fear in ourselves belong to the dark, shadowy background of the unconscious. If we cannot face and accept them, we become divided people. In saying that it is not the deed, but the thought itself that is sinful, Paul's ethic puts mankind in an intolerable position.

An interesting contrast to Paul's idea of what makes a holy man can be found in the writings of the Sioux Indian holy man, Lame Deer, who writes:

> Sickness, jail, poverty, getting drunk—I had to experience all that myself. Sinning makes the world go round. You can't be so stuck up, so inhuman that you want to be pure, your soul wrapped up in a plastic bag, all the time. You have to be God and the devil, both of them. Being a good medicine man means being right in the midst of the turmoil, not shielding yourself from it. It means experiencing life in all its phases. It means not being afraid of cutting up and playing the fool now and then. That's sacred too.[9]

And elsewhere he notes:

> White people pay a preacher to be "good," to behave himself in public, to wear a collar, to keep away from a certain kind of woman. But nobody pays an Indian medicine man to be good, to behave himself and act respectable. The *wicasa wakan* (holy man) just acts like himself. He has been given the freedom—the freedom of a tree or a bird. That freedom can be beautiful or ugly; it doesn't matter much.[10]

Paul's attitude toward women and the persona is found in the First Epistle of Timothy. After putting women in their place as inferior to men, Paul adds: "Nevertheless, she will be saved by childbearing, provided she lives a modest life and is constant in faith and love and holiness." [11]

Such a passage makes us wonder what happened to salvation through Christ. Since women are saved by childbearing and a modest life, we have to assume that salvation through Christ is reserved only for men. Nor are we told what happens to women who are unable for one reason or another to have children, or who are called upon to lead a different life from the life of motherhood. As for the holy life women are to live, that obviously does not leave a woman the right to a Shadow. For who can always be "constant in faith, love, and holiness?" What does a woman do when anger, resentment, frustration, boredom, or just plain exhaustion get the better of her? Anyone who has had the task of raising small children knows how impossible it is always to be a model of holiness, and how dark one's emotions can become from time to time under the burden of parenthood, or the stress of living with an unrelated spouse. But Paul offers a woman no alternative but to resolutely cut off all the dark side of herself, and to feel bad about herself if it should show up. Not only is this impossible, it is not even desirable. A woman, like a man, needs the dark side of herself in order to become an individual. Moreover, it is not anger as such that injures children, but repressed, unrecognized anger. Children instinctively understand anger when it is expressed in a related way, but they cannot stand the kind of rejection that occurs in parents who are unable to face their dark side.

I do not mean to be too hard on Paul. He made many positive contributions to Christian life, and in most respects was a remarkable and exemplary person. Furthermore, it is not Paul himself who is to blame for the one–sided attitudes I have illustrated, but the early Church generally. Paul says these things because this is the prevailing attitude of the early Church which he represents. The problem is not that Paul is such a bad person, but that he was an historically conditioned personality who, however inspired he might have been in certain respects, did not go beyond the prevailing collective opinions with regard to the psychological problem of the persona and the Shadow. Jesus was sufficiently conscious that he was able to transcend the collective thinking of his time. Paul was not able to do this. It is unfortunate that the Church elected to follow the admonitions of Paul rather than the teaching of Jesus in this regard. But that was inevitable. Given the general level of consciousness of the Church, it was certain that the teachings of Jesus would be disregarded, and the words of Paul would be followed, for this is where people were at that time. Nevertheless it is unfortunate, for a great deal of psychological damage could have been avoided had the teachings of Jesus been followed with regard to the dynamics of human personality.

We have seen that Jesus knew of the persona and that he spoke out against the spiritual danger of identification with a mask. In the quotation from Matthew that we have already considered, we saw that Jesus compared people who are identified with the persona with a whitewashed tomb that looks pure on the outside but inside is full of dirt and corruption. As we noted, this inner corruption is like the shadow personality when seen in contrast to a persona. The question is how to relate to the Shadow. We have seen that to repress it is no solution, but neither can we identify with the Shadow and live out all of our impulses and darkness. This would not be integration or a solution of the problem, but would simply be a move from one opposite to the other. The inner split would still remain. Fortunately Jesus did give us some guidelines on how to deal with the problem. Consider this verse from Matthew: "Come to terms with your opponent in good time while you are still on the way to the court with him, or he may hand you over to the judge and the judge to the officer, and you will be thrown into prison. I tell you solemnly, you will not get out till you have paid the last penny." [12] In those days it was the custom for disputants in a legal case to journey to the court in company with each other in the hope that they might settle the dispute enroute and not have to trouble the judge. So we might take this saying of Jesus as advice that this custom be followed. The difficulty with this interpretation is that it is hardly worth saying; it would have been commonplace advice anyone could have given. There is also the difficulty of the last sentence: if we do not do this, Jesus says, the judge will send us to prison.

The passage makes excellent sense, however, if we take it psychologically. In this case the opponent with whom we must come to terms is in *us;* it is the shadow personality that opposes our persona and to which we must somehow relate, and Jesus is telling us that our job is to make peace with this inner adversary during our lifetime. If we do not, there will be a final reckoning and *we* will be found wanting. Notice that it is not the adversary, the Shadow, who will be punished, but the ego. It is the task of consciousness to face, recognize and try to be reconciled with, all aspects of our personality. This is our psychological work or *opus,* and if we fail to assume this task for ourselves we are evidently found wanting by God.

The punishment Jesus speaks of in his image is that of being thrown into prison until the last penny is paid. The process of becoming a psychologically conscious person, and relating all aspects of our personality to our conscious life, is of crucial importance; we refuse this life task only at our peril. It is hard work to become a conscious person, but the price to be paid if we remain unconscious is much greater.

Another well-known passage from Jesus about the shadow problem is the parable of the Prodigal Son, found in Luke 15:11–32.

> A man had two sons. The younger said to his father, "Father, let me have the share of the estate that would come to me." So the father divided the property between them. A few days later, the younger son got together everything he had and left for a distant country where he squandered his money on a life of debauchery.
>
> When he had spent it all, that country experienced a severe famine, and now he began to feel the pinch, so he hired himself out to one of the local inhabitants who put him on his farm to feed the pigs. And he would willingly have filled his belly with the husks the pigs were eating but no one offered him anything. Then he came to his senses and said, "How many of my father's paid servants have more food than they want, and here am I dying of hunger! I will leave this place and go to my father and say: Father, I have sinned against heaven and against you; I no longer deserve to be called your son; treat me as one of your paid servants." So he left the place and went back to his father.
>
> While he was still a long way off, his father saw him and was

moved with pity. He ran to the boy, clasped him in his arms and kissed him tenderly. Then his son said, "Father, I have sinned against heaven and against you. I no longer deserve to be called your son." But the father said to his servants, "Quick! Bring out the best robe and put it on him; put a ring on his finger and sandals on his feet. Bring the calf we have been fattening, and kill it; we are going to have a feast, a celebration, because this son of mine was dead and has come back to life; he was lost and is found." And they began to celebrate.

Now the elder son was out in the fields and on his way back, as he drew near the house, he could hear music and dancing. Calling one of the servants he asked what it was all about. "Your brother has come" replied the servant "and your father has killed the calf we had fattened because he has got him back safe and sound." He was angry then and refused to go in, and his father came out to plead with him; but he answered his father, "Look, all these years I have slaved for you and never once disobeyed your orders, yet you never offered me so much as a kid for me to celebrate with my friends. But, for this son of yours, when he comes back after swallowing up your property—he and his women—you kill the calf we had been fattening." The father said, "My son, you are with me always and all I have is yours. But it was only right we should celebrate and rejoice, because your brother here was dead and has come to life; he was lost and is found."

Again we see the problem of man's duality. All of us have within us an elder brother, who conforms to social expectations, and a younger brother, a shadow side who wants to "live it out." The consequences of acting out this shadow side are disastrous; the prodigal son's behaviour only leads him to ruin. But at the crucial moment the younger son becomes conscious. The parable tells us that he "came to himself." To "come to oneself" is to see the Shadow, the dark reality of who we are, and this is the moment when salvation and wholeness are possible.

The parable concludes with the attempt of the father to reconcile the two hostile sons through his own loving attitude. It is not clear whether the hard heart of the elder brother was melted and he accepted his younger brother or not. Had he done so, it would have amounted to an inner reconciliation of the two halves of the personality, the establishment of a saving bridge between the social, conforming side and the rebellious Shadow.

In suggesting that the parable is capable of this subjective psychological interpretation I am not saying that this is the only level on which the parable has meaning. The beauty of the teachings of Jesus is that most of what he said has meaning on many levels: the social, ethical, theological, and psychological. But it is the psychological meaning that has been largely neglected and which concerns us here.

One reason that the problem of the Shadow has been ignored by the Church is that it leads us to paradoxical situations and confronts us with the need for a paradoxical ethic. We do not like paradoxes, and traditional Christian consciousness in particular prefers things to be spelled out in black and white. Unfortunately, the acceptance of our shadow side does not permit this, for the Shadow, with all of its potentiality for evil, also contains what is necessary for the highest good of all: wholeness. This is why a discussion of the Shadow always leads to a paradox.

An example of this is found in Luke 7:36–50, a story we have already commented on briefly. In this engaging story Jesus is dining with one of the Pharisees when a woman with a bad reputation comes in to him, weeps, and cleans his feet with her tears. The Pharisee watches all this in amazement and says to himself that if only Jesus knew who this woman was he would have nothing to do with her. Jesus intuits what the Pharisee is thinking and challenges him. Suppose there were two people, he says, each of whom owed a creditor a sum of money, one owing him twice what the other owed. Then suppose the creditor forgave them both. Who would be more grateful? The Pharisee has to answer that the one who was forgiven the most would love his creditor more than the other.

This, says Jesus, is the way it is with this woman. He points out that when he came to the Pharisee's house no one poured water over his feet, but this woman washed them with her tears because of her love and gratitude. He then makes this paradoxical statement: "For this reason I tell you that her sins, her many sins, must have been forgiven her, or she would not have shown such great love. It is the man who is forgiven little who shows little love." Then to the woman he adds, "Your faith has saved you; go in peace."

The paradox of what Jesus is saying confounds any attempt to see things in black and white. To live out our shadow side, as this woman did, is to commit many sins. Jesus makes it clear that in his view this woman had to change her way of life. On the other hand, to play it safe, as did the Pharisee, and remain unaware of the potentiality for sin in us and our need for forgiveness, is to become cut off from our capacity for compassion and love. If we only play it safe in life, we never come to know who we are; life must be thoroughly lived if we are to become whole people, and it is better to be forgiven than to be self–righteous.

Jesus' point of view is perhaps best summed up in a frequently misunderstood verse in Matthew 5:48: "You must therefore be perfect just as your heavenly father is perfect." The problem here is that most English readers miss the significance of the Greek word translated "perfect." Perfect, for us, means without blemish, stain, or spot; it suggests the kind of blameless perfection Paul urges on his Christian converts; that is, a life in which they never have any earthy, angry or selfish thoughts or desires. Such a life, as we have seen, is a psychological impossibility, and if we strive for this kind of perfection it only creates a split in us. But the Greek wording of Matthew 5:48 does not refer to purity, but to completion. The word translated "perfect" in English is the Greek word *teleios*, which means brought to completion. It is derived from the Greek word *telos*, which means the end or goal and is the word from which we get our word *teleology*, which is that branch of philosophy that studies the final goal of life. Literally the verse is to be translated, "Be you therefore ones brought to completion even as your heavenly father is complete."

What Jesus is urging, then, is that our lives and personalities are to be brought to completeness, to the end goal for which they are destined. This will necessarily involve recognition of the Shadow and the acceptance of this part of ourselves as an inevitable part of our totality. The solution to the shadow problem that Jesus suggests, then, involves the growth of psychological consciousness and spiritual maturity by the recognition of our dark side as well as of our light side; he does *not* call upon us to repress the Shadow and identify with a persona.

So the essential difference between the teachings of Paul and those of Jesus can be said to be this: Paul urges us to a one–sided expression of "goodness"; Jesus urges us to become complete or whole. Paul's psychological ethic can only be accomplished by repression, that is, by a systematic unconsciousness of the Shadow. Jesus' ethic can only be fulfilled by becoming conscious of the Shadow, enduring the resulting tension, and undergoing the developmental process that can proceed only when consciousness of the Shadow has been reached. Paul's attitude, as we have seen, is expressive of the general attitude of his times. Throughout the centuries the Church has not departed significantly from it. In this regard, the Church has not lived up to the higher consciousness of Jesus but has remained on a lower psychological level. The result has been a perpetuation of man's split and the aggravation, rather than resolution, of the problem of the Shadow.

This is why the New Testament ends where it does: with the Book of Revelation. For in this book there is a metaphysical cleavage and duality between God and Satan that is a mirror of the unsolved problem of man's own soul. Gone is the blessedness of the Jesus of the Gospels whose attitude was able to unite the opposites, and instead we have a stridently one–sided figure of goodness who is certain to constellate its opposite. In Revelation we see revealed not God's ultimate nature, but man's unresolved problem projected into the metaphysical realm.

Of course many people will object to such an interpretation of Jesus' teaching and will prefer the relative clarity and simplicity of the Pauline viewpoint. For one thing, we are not used to seeing the psychological dimension of Christianity. For another, it seems that Jesus' path is far too difficult, and that it is unreasonable to expect mankind to follow it. Jesus himself saw that his way was not easy: "The road that leads to perdition is wide and spacious, and many take it; but it is a narrow gate and a hard road that leads to life, and only a few find it." [13]

There is no doubt that the path prescribed for us by Jesus is a way that makes great demands on us. To become psychologically conscious, and to face honestly the duality in oneself, can be difficult and painful. It is not surprising that, almost from the beginning, those who adopted Jesus' name managed to avoid seeing the consequences of his teaching in this regard. For Jesus' way is an individual way. It can never be accomplished collectively or en masse. That is why he likens it to the "narrow gate," for only one person at a time can pass through a narrow gate; in contrast, the multitude can go down the wide and spacious road that leads to perdition. As soon as anyone has recognized his or her personal Shadow, that personality has begun the path to individual consciousness; in spite of its painfulness, that is the narrow gate that leads to life.

Still, it might be argued that the common run of humanity can hardly be expected to fulfill Jesus' demanding psychological ethic. Left to themselves, it can be said, people will surely indulge in sin, waste their lives, and deny their Creator. Far better to tell them what to do, how to act, and what to avoid, than to admonish them to an increased psychological awareness that most people do not want.

This point of view has been eloquently argued by the Grand Inquisitor in a chapter by that name in Dostoevsky's novel *The Brothers Karamazov.* In this fantasy the Christ has returned, but far from being greeted with joy by the Grand Inquisitor, who is the leader of the Church that bears Christ's name, he has been imprisoned. In prison Christ is visited by the old man, who accuses him of having come back to disturb and disrupt the work that the Church has carried on in his name. The Church, says the Grand Inquisitor, has "corrected" Christ's work. Christ placed on mankind an impossible demand that they be free people, which was certain to make them miserable, and which only a few could fulfill anyway. Fortunately, the Church saw man's plight and made the necessary corrections in Jesus' teachings. The Church had man's happiness in mind—Christ did not—and so lifted the burden of freedom from him. Now, says the Grand Inquisitor, Christ has no right to come back and add anything to what he has said of old.

The Grand Inquisitor exists wherever men substitute a collective, unconscious way of life for the free ethic of Jesus. The State can become the Grand Inquisitor when it takes away the freedom of the individual, even though it does this in the name of the happiness of its people. The Church, too, can be the Grand Inquisitor, and Paul, without realizing it, started the process when he handed to his Christian congregations the requirement that they be good rather than conscious.

As Dostoevsky makes clear, the destructive element in the attitude of the Grand Inquisitor is that he takes away man's freedom. Jesus' ethic, though demanding, does not take away man's freedom. Freedom, which involves the necessity that we assume the burden of psychological choice and conflict, runs throughout everything Jesus said and did. When the prodigal son decided to waste his life, the father in the parable did not try to stop him, nor did God interfere with the freedom of the woman who washed Jesus' feet, to lead a life of sin. And when the rich young man went away sorrowfully after Jesus told him he must sell all he had and give to the poor, the story does not tell us that Jesus ran down the street after him urging him to change his mind.[14] The greatest ethical value, according to Jesus, is to become a free person, and this means being a conscious person.

Paul's ethic takes away man's freedom. When we are told to conform to a standard of goodness imposed upon us by collective authority, and to repress everything from our consciousness that contradicts this, we have lost our freedom; we are no longer expected to be conscious people, responsible for ourselves. But in Jesus' ethic man is left with the alternatives life poses to him, the problem of his own duality and the necessity for psychological honesty. Growth in consciousness is valued more highly by Jesus than conformity to "goodness." Freedom is of the highest psychological value, because this alone makes possible the development of consciousness and love. It may well be that this is why we are created with such dual natures, since duality is the precondition of conscious psychological development.

Notes

[1] Matt. 23:27–28.

[2] Rom. 7:14–26.

[3] Other passages that are concerned with the persona–Shadow problem include: 1 Cor. 4:5, 5:1–3; Rom. 1:18–32, 2:8, 2:21, 13:11–14, 12:9–21, 16:19–29; Phil. 1:11, 2:3–5, 2:15; Col. 3:5–25; Eph. 5:2–20; 1 Tim. 1:8–11; Titus 1:5–9.

[4] Gal. 5:16–24 and 6:9–10.

[5] Rom. 12:17–19.

[6] Rom. 13:14.

[7] Cf. 1 Cor. 7:1–11.

[8] 1 Tim. 3:2–7. It is a matter of scholarly dispute, of course, whether or not Paul wrote First Timothy. Conservative Roman Catholic scholars and Bishop J. A. T. Robinson, in his *Redating the New Testament* (Philadelphia: Westminster, 1976), believes that he did. Other modern scholars believe that he did not. For reasons that are made clear on page 86, it is not too important who authored First Timothy since Paul's views and those of the early Church generally do not differ much with regard to the problem of the Shadow.

[9] John Fire/Lame Deer and Richard Erdoes, *Lame Deer—Seeker of Visions* (New York: Simon & Schuster, 1972), p. 79.

[10] *Ibid.*, p. 156.

[11] 1 Tim. 2:15. Cf. Tim. 2:9–15; 5:3–8.

[12] Matt. 5:25–26.

[13] Matt. 7:13–14.

[14] Matt. 19:16–22.

CHAPTER SEVEN

The Problem of the Shadow and Evil in *The Strange Case of Dr. Jekyll and Mr. Hyde*

A brilliant study of evil and the Shadow is found in Robert Louis Stevenson's novelette *The Strange Case of Dr. Jekyll and Mr. Hyde.* Written about 1886, this exciting mystery story tells us about mankind's dual nature in a way that is especially remarkable since Stevenson's story anticipated Freud by over a decade and Jung by more than that.

The Strange Case of Dr. Jekyll and Mr. Hyde is a story that few people have read but with which almost everyone is familiar. "Jekyll and Hyde" have become part of our common parlance so that everyone knows, for example, what it means when a magazine headline reads: "Was the Hillside Strangler a Jekyll and Hyde?" [1] It is unfortunate that more people have not actually read the tale, for not only is it an interesting story in its own right, well told by a clever storyteller, it is also full of psychological insight into the problem of the Shadow. The story must have been especially exciting when it was first read by its English and American audience in the late nineteenth century, for it is a mystery story, and the key to the mystery—that Jekyll and Hyde are one and the same person—is only revealed to the reader at the very end.

When a story has found its way into the common mind, so that almost everyone has heard of it and is aware of its central theme, we may be sure that it is because the tale has an archetypal quality. In this case the archetype involved in that of the Shadow, and "Jekyll and Hyde" has lodged itself firmly in our common imagination. Somewhere in our hearts we know that there is a Jekyll and Hyde within us too, and this is so even though we have no personal insight into our own Shadow. For the archetypes are so numinous, that is, so charged with emotional energy, that they fascinate us even if we do not comprehend them.

The archetypal nature of the tale is further exemplified in the manner in which the story came to be written. In his autobiographical book *Across the Plains*,[2] Stevenson tells us how he wrote his stories. He was greatly assisted, he tells us, by his "little people" or "Brownies," to whom he always turned for help when the need for money, and hence another story, became pressing. His "Sleepless Brownies," he says, do him "honest service," and fashion for him better tales than he could ever fashion for himself. They labor all night long if need be, even in his dreams, to devise plots and characters and fill his imagination with the necessary clues from which to fabricate his tales. So it was with *The Strange Case of Dr. Jekyll and Mr. Hyde.* "I had long been trying to write a story on this subject," Stevenson tells us, "to find a body, a vehicle, for that strong sense of man's double being which must at times come in upon and overwhelm the mind of every thinking creature. . . . For two days I went about racking my brains for a plot of any sort; and on the second night I dreamed the scene at the window, and a scene afterwards split in two, in which Hyde, pursued for some crime, took the powder and underwent the change in the presence of his pursuers." Evidently Stevenson first *dreamt* of Jekyll and Hyde, so that the theme for the story was directly provided by the unconscious itself.

To what extent Stevenson's dream of Hyde, and his general preoccupation with the problem of the Shadow, is a reflection of his own personal psychological struggles, and to what extent Stevenson, as an artist, is preoccupied with a problem of general human concern, we will not dwell upon here, though the interested student may want to read Barbara Hannah's excellent study of Stevenson in her book *Striving for Wholeness*.[3] What will concern us is the tale, and what it has to tell us of the problem of the Shadow and of evil. Because many of us may not have read the story, or may have read it some time ago, I am including a synopsis of the tale. The reader already familiar with the story may wish to move directly to the commentary on the story which follows the synopsis.

Synopsis of *The Strange Case of Dr. Jekyll and Mr. Hyde*

The story begins with a lawyer, Mr. Utterson, stumbling into the mystery of the strange door. Mr. Utterson, described as "lean, long, dusty, dreary, and yet somehow lovable," is taking his once-a-week walk with his friend, Mr. Richard Enfield, "well-known man about town." On this particular occasion their way took them to a "by-street in a busy quarter of London." Here there was a mysterious door, with no bell or knocker, "blistered and distained," carved up by shoolboys and in general disrepair, yet no one had appeared for a generation to repair these ravages. "Did you ever remark that door?" Enfield asks the unassuming Mr. Utterson, and then proceeds to tell a strange tale. Enfield was coming home late one night when all at once he saw a young, powerfully built little man stumping along at a great rate and, coming the other direction, a little girl running hard down the cross street. The two met, but the man knocked the girl over and calmly proceeded to trample over her body, leaving her screaming on the ground. "It was hellish to see," Enfield related, "It wasn't like a man; it was like some damned Juggernaut." The girl had cried out, and her screams brought people running, including Enfield, who ran after the culprit and brought him back to the awful scene. The girl proved to be unhurt, but there was something about the little man that aroused the fury of the onlookers. Enfield saw a doctor who had been summoned "turn sick and white with the desire to kill him." And the women were "wild as harpies." "I never saw a circle of such hateful faces," Enfield related, "and there was the man in the middle with a kind of black, sneering coolness . . . . carrying it off, sir, really like Satan." Since killing the man is out of the question, the crowd demands reparations from him for the sake of the child's family, and the ugly man finally agrees to pay 100 pounds. He then produces a key, goes through the strange door, and soon emerges with a check, which proved to be genuine, for the required amount of money. The check was signed by a well-known man in the town, a man, Enfield related, who "is the very pink of the proprieties. . . . one of your fellows who do what they call good." Enfield supposed it to be a case of blackmail, that the ugly man had something on the good man, from the latter's youth perhaps, and, out of respect for the good man's name in town, Enfield refrained from asking more questions.

Utterson is left deep in thought. "There's one point I want to ask," he says, ". . . the name of that man who walked over the child."

"It was a man of the name of Hyde," Enfield replies. "He is not easy to describe. There is something wrong with his appearance; something displeasing, something downright detestable. I never saw a man I so disliked, and yet I scarce know why. He must be deformed somewhere; he gives a strong feeling of deformity, although I couldn't specify the point."

Mr. Utterson is shocked, for he knows the name already of the man who signed the cheque! As we will soon see, the man is Utterson's client, the respected Dr. Henry Jekyll. The two friends make an agreement never to refer to the matter again, and Utterson thoughtfully returns home, goes to his safe, and pulls out Dr. Henry Jekyll's will. This strange document, drawn up only by the doctor, for Utterson refused to have anything to do with it, orders that in the event of his disappearance for three months, all of Jekyll's goods are to be bestowed without question upon Hyde. The will had been detestable to Utterson before, but now that he knows Hyde to be such a sinister and despicable character it seems to him worse and more inexplicable than ever.

In his agitation Utterson goes to the house of Dr. Lanyon, a mutual friend of Dr. Jekyll and himself, where he inquires if Dr. Lanyon knows of the mysterious Hyde. But all that Utterson learns from Lanyon is that the two doctors, who once were close friends, have now drawn apart. "It is more than ten years since Henry Jekyll became too fanciful for me," Lanyon tells Utterson. "He began to go wrong, wrong in my mind . . . I see and I have seen devilish little of the man. Such unscientific balderdash," Lanyon exclaims, his face "flushing suddenly purple."

Utterson returns home but can no longer sleep. In his tortured mind he keeps seeing the apparition of Mr. Hyde, but, of course, he has never seen his face. If he could only see Hyde, Utterson thinks to himself, then perhaps the mystery would lighten and he could sleep once more. So Utterson begins to frequent the area around the mysterious door that leads into Jekyll's laboratory and, at last, his efforts are rewarded as he sees a young, deformed looking little man approach the door and brandish a key.

"Mr. Utterson stepped out and touched him on the shoulder as he passed. 'Mr. Hyde, I think?'

"Mr. Hyde shrank back with a hissing intake of the breath. But his fear was only momentary; and though he did not look the lawyer in the face, he answered coolly enough; 'That is my name. What do you want?'

" 'I see you are going in,' returned the lawyer. 'I am an old friend of Dr. Jekyll's—Mr. Utterson of Gaunt Street—you must have heard my name; and meeting you so conveniently, I thought you might admit me.'

" 'You will not find Dr. Jekyll; he is from home,' replied Mr. Hyde, blowing in the key. And then suddenly, but still without looking up, 'How did you know me?' he asked.

" 'On your side,' said Mr. Utterson, 'will you do me a favour?'

" 'With pleasure,' replied the other, 'What shall it be?'

" 'Will you let me see your face?' asked the lawyer.

"Mr. Hyde appeared to hesitate, and then, as if upon some sudden reflection, fronted about with an air of defiance; and the pair stared at each other pretty fixedly for a few seconds. 'Now I shall know you again,' said Mr. Utterson, 'it may be useful.'

" 'Yes,' returned Mr. Hyde, 'it is as well we have met; and à propos, you should have my address.' And he gave a number of a street in Soho.

" 'Good God!' thought Mr. Utterson, 'can he, too, have been thinking of the will?' But he kept his feelings to himself and only grunted in acknowledgment of the address.

" 'And now,' said the other, 'how did you know me?'

" 'By description,' was the reply.

" 'Whose description?'

" 'We have common friends,' said Mr. Utterson.

" 'Common friends?' echoed Mr. Hyde, a little hoarsely. 'Who are they?'

" 'Jekyll, for instance,' said the lawyer.

" 'He never told you,' cried Mr. Hyde, with a flush of anger. 'I did not think you would have lied.'

" 'Come,' said Mr. Utterson, 'that is not fitting language.'

"The other snarled aloud with a savage laugh; and the next moment, with extraordinary quickness, he had unlocked the door and disappeared into the house."

Mr. Utterson has seen Hyde, but his mind is no more at ease than before, for ugly though Hyde was, nothing "could explain the hitherto unknown disgust, loathing, and fear with which Mr. Utterson regarded him. 'O my poor old Harry Jekyll,' Utterson says to himself, 'if ever I read Satan's signature upon a face, it is on that of your new friend.' "

So Utterson decides to go and visit Henry Jekyll. He is recognized and allowed in by the butler, Poole, but Dr. Jekyll is out. Utterson thinks this especially strange since he knows Hyde to have entered by the side door, but Poole tells him that though the servants practically never see Hyde, they have instructions to obey him, and that Hyde often leaves and enters through the laboratory door.

Utterson is hardly reassured by this knowledge. As he trudges home he thinks that Jekyll must be in great trouble. Surely, he supposes, the ugly Mr. Hyde is able for some reason to blackmail Jekyll. Moreover, what if Hyde learns of the will which leaves everything to him? Mischief must be the result of that! Utterson decides he must help his friend Henry Jekyll. " 'If Jekyll will but let me, if Jekyll will only let me.' "

Two weeks later Utterson is invited to a dinner party and finally has the opportunity to talk with Jekyll. So for the first time in the tale we meet with the central figure of Henry Jekyll, who is described as a "large, well made, smooth-faced man of fifty, with something of a slyish cast perhaps, but every mark of capacity and kindness—you could see by his looks that he cherished for Mr. Utterson a sincere and warm affection."

Utterson manages to remain until after the other guests have departed and at last is able to talk with his friend and client about the matter of his will, and of the mysterious Mr. Hyde. But he receives little satisfaction. Regarding the will, Jekyll does not want to discuss the matter, but when Hyde's name is brought up, and Utterson tells how he has met the man, "The large handsome face of Dr. Jekyll grew pale to the very lips, and there came a blackness about his eyes. 'I do not care to hear more,' said he. 'This is a matter I thought we had agreed to drop.' "

Utterson persists, and Jekyll declares that his relationship with Hyde is indeed painful, and his position is strange, but that it is a matter that "cannot be mended by talking." When Utterson urges Jekyll to trust him, Jekyll says he is appreciative, but he can only tell Utterson one thing: "the moment I choose, I can be rid of Mr. Hyde." The conversation concludes with Jekyll asking for and receiving a pledge from his friend, Utterson, to help Hyde when and if Jekyll should no longer be here, for, Jekyll declares, "I do sincerely take a great, a very great interest in that young man."

But Utterson does learn one thing: that Jekyll and Dr. Lanyon have had a more serious falling out than he had supposed. Jekyll refers to Lanyon as "that hide–bound pedant . . . an ignorant, blatant pedant." He is angry at Lanyon because Lanyon objects to what he calls Jekyll's "scientific heresies." Jekyll concludes, "I was never more disappointed in any man than Lanyon."

Defeated in his efforts to get to the bottom of the mystery of Mr. Hyde, Utterson is forced to silence. But a year later an event happens which not only shocks the whole of London by its "singular ferocity" but also reawakens in Utterson his need to get to the bottom of the mystery of the strange relationship between Dr. Jekyll and Mr. Hyde. One late evening, a maid, looking out of her window, sees an old man walking along the street, and, coming the other way, an ugly young man with a cane, whom she recognizes, from a visit he once made to her master, as a certain Mr. Hyde, and for whom she had conceived an instant dislike. When the two met on the street the young man suddenly began to beat the old man unmercifully with the cane, clubbing him to the earth, and trampling him underfoot until the old man's bones were audibly shattered. The maid fainted, and when she awoke the old man was lying there dead on the sidewalk, the murderer long gone, but one half of the cane with which the deed had been done lay there in the gutter—the other, no doubt, having been carried away. The police were summoned, and a purse, gold watch, and letter were found upon the victim's body. The letter bore the name of Mr. Utterson.

The next morning Mr. Utterson was visited by the police, and he was able to identify the old man as his client, the well–known and highly regarded London personality Sir Danvers Carew. When he was told that the maid identified the assailant as one Mr. Hyde he was shocked, but when he was shown the broken cane he turned pale for he recognized the cane as one that he himself gave to his friend, Henry Jekyll, several years before.

Of course Mr. Utterson has Hyde's address, and takes the police to the address in Soho, a dismal quarter of the city. "This was the home of Henry Jekyll's favourite; of a man who was heir to quarter of a million sterling." They knock at the door of the apartment and an evil–faced old woman answers, and grudgingly tells them that this was Mr. Hyde's apartment, but he had left less than an hour ago. The police enter the apartment and find that it was furnished in luxury and in good taste, but that the rooms had obviously been recently ransacked, for clothes are strewn every which way, and there are piles of papers which had been hastily burned. In the debris the police find the butt end of a green cheque book, which had resisted the fire, and the other half of the cane. The police think that now surely they can find the culprit; they need only wait by the bank for him to appear to draw his cash. But the matter does not prove so easy. He had no family, there were no photographs, only a few people had ever seen him, and on only one point could people agree regarding his description: that there was about him a "haunting sense of unexpressed deformity." So Hyde seems for the time being to have effected a complete and total escape.

Mr. Utterson, filled again with anxiety for his friend, goes once more to Jekyll's house where is is admitted by Poole and is led to the doctor's laboratory, the first time he had ever been received in this part of the house. Here he is greeted by his friend, but it is not the ebullient doctor of old, but a Dr. Jekyll who looks deathly sick, who does not rise to meet his visitor, but holds out a cold hand and welcomes him in a changed voice. "You have not been mad enough to hide this fellow?" asks Utterson as the conversation soon centers on the tragic murder and the hunted Hyde. "Utterson," says Jekyll, "I swear to God, I swear to God I will never set eyes on him again. I bind my honour to you that I am done with him in this world. It is all at an end. And indeed he does not want my help; you do not know him as I do; he is safe, he is quite safe; mark my words, he will never more be heard of."

Later in the conversation Utterson offers the thought to Jekyll that Hyde meant to murder him and get the proceeds from the will. "You have had a fine escape," Utterson declares. "I have had what is far more to the purpose," returned the doctor solemnly, "I have had a lesson—O God, Utterson, what a lesson I have had!" And he covered his face for a moment with his hands.

Utterson is somewhat reassured, though he marvels at his friend's strange behaviour, but before he leaves, Henry Jekyll gives him a letter to read, a letter he had received from Hyde himself which signified briefly that Dr. Jekyll had more than repaid Hyde what he owed to him and that he, Hyde, had a means of escape on which he placed a sure dependence. Jekyll asks Utterson for his advice, and Utterson leaves with the letter to deliberate the matter. But, moved by a strange inspiration, Utterson takes the letter to his friend, Mr. Guest, who is a handwriting expert. By chance a second letter, from Jekyll himself, falls into their hands and Mr. Guest compares the two handwritings. They are, he concludes, from the same hand, differing only in slope, but with a singular resemblance. Utterson is shocked: " 'Henry Jekyll forge for a murderer!' he says to himself. And his blood ran cold in his veins."

So the mystery deepens, and time goes by, and there is no sign of Mr. Hyde. True, news came out of his vile life, of his callousness and violence, and the hatred he received from all who knew him. But he himself has disappeared, and with the disappearance everyone gradually begins to relax. There was also a new life for Henry Jekyll. He came out of seclusion, renewed his friendship with Utterson and Lanyon, became even more dedicated to good works, and "was now no less distinguished for religion" as well.

And so it was for more than two months, until one day Utterson, who had been a daily visitor at his friend's house, found the door at Jekyll's shut against him. "The doctor was confined to the house," Poole the butler told him, "and saw no one." Again and again Utterson was turned away until at last he went to consult Dr. Lanyon about the matter, only to find Lanyon was at death's door. It was not simply his physical deterioration that shook Utterson, it was also "a look in the eye and quality of manner that seemed to testify to some deep-seated terror of the mind." When Utterson brings up the matter of Jekyll, Lanyon bursts into a tirade. "I wish to see or hear no more of Dr. Jekyll!" he exclaims. He can give Utterson no explanation, but only reiterates that nothing can be done and that he wishes to hear no more of "this accursed topic."

Baffled, Utterson returns home and writes to Jekyll inquiring about the unhappy break with Lanyon, and complaining that he has been excluded from the house. He learns in a reply from Jekyll that the quarrel with Lanyon is incurable: "I do not blame our old friend," Jekyll wrote, "but I share his view that we must never meet. I mean from henceforth to lead a life of extreme seclusion; you must not be surprised, nor must you doubt my friendship, if my door is often shut even to you. You must suffer me to go my own dark way. I have brought on myself a punishment and a danger that I cannot name."

Shortly after this Lanyon dies. Greatly affected, Utterson, the night following the funeral, takes from its locked place a letter, carefully sealed, entrusted to him by Lanyon shortly before his death, and inscribed, "Private: for the hands of G. J. Utterson alone, and in case of his predecease *to be destroyed unread.*"

Reluctantly, Utterson breaks open the seal and, inside, finds another enclosure, marked upon the cover "not to be opened till the death or disappearance of Dr. Henry Jekyll." Here it was again, the allusion to the possible disappearance of Henry Jekyll! Before it had been a notation in Jekyll's will. Now it was inscribed on the inner packet in the handwriting of the dead Dr. Lanyon. Professional ethics restrain Utterson from opening the packet and inspecting its contents and the unread missive is locked away again.

Utterson continues to try to see his friend Jekyll but is consistently turned away and gradually becomes discouraged. Poole tells him that the doctor is now more confined than ever, and that he seldom leaves the laboratory, has grown silent, is out of spirits, and that it seems always as if something is on his mind. Like the master storyteller he is, Stevenson lays out for the reader the many pieces of the puzzle that must all be put together: the mysterious relationship of Jekyll and Hyde, Hyde's almost miraculous disappearance, Jekyll's visible decline and total seclusion after two months of a changed life, Lanyon's inexplicable death, the unexplained break between the two friends, the "forged" letter, the mysterious packet not to be opened until Jekyll's death or disappearance that came to Utterson via Lanyon before his death, and now Jekyll's unexplainable seclusion.

With no encouragement from Jekyll to renew his visits, Utterson gradually loses energy to solve the mystery, until one day a shocking incident occurs that sets his mind aflame once again. It happened one Sunday, when Mr. Utterson and Mr. Enfield were on their customary walk, that their way once more took them to the by–street in London where lay the mysterious door that led to Dr. Jekyll's laboratory. Just when the two friends were congratulating themselves that the mysterious matter of Hyde had come to an end, they chanced to see Dr. Jekyll framed in the window of the building like a "disconsolate prisoner." The two friends greeted him with enthusiasm, and for a short while Jekyll returned their warm greetings, almost, so it seemed, accepting their invitation to come down and visit, when "the smile was struck out of his face and succeeded by an expression of such abject terror and despair, as froze the very blood of the two gentlemen below." The window was slammed down, and the two friends below looked at each other with horror in their eyes. "God forgive us, God forgive us," said Mr. Utterson. And silently they walked away.

Shortly after this came the last night. Utterson was seated by his fireside when he had an unexpected visitor: Poole, the butler, who had come because he thought foul play had been done to his master, urges Utterson to accompany him home. Utterson does so, and is greeted with relief by the servants, amongst whom is a frightened housemaid, who breaks into "hysterical whimpering." Taking Utterson to the laboratory door, Poole calls out, "Mr. Utterson, sir, asking to see you." A voice answers from within, "Tell him I cannot see any one," but the voice was not that of Jekyll! Back in the main quarters of the house Poole explains that all week there has been a crying night and day from whoever is in the laboratory for some kind of medicine, and two or three times a

day the butler finds written instructions cast outside the laboratory door for Poole to go to this apothecary or that to find a pure
version of a drug that is wanted badly, but no matter how many
times the prescription is filled it turns out to be unsatisfactory to
whoever it is who is in the laboratory waiting in such despera-
tion. And once, Poole relates, he saw the creature himself, as he
had slipped out to look for the latest drug brought back from the
chemist, the figure of a man with a mask upon his face. "If it was
my master," cried out Poole to Utterson, "why did he cry out like
a rat, and run from me?" There was someone in the laboratory,
someone strange, for "Once," said Poole, "I heard it weeping,
weeping like a woman or a lost soul."

Reluctantly the two men conclude that Jekyll has probably
been murdered, and that the mysterious intruder can be none
other than Edward Hyde; they now feel that they have no choice
but to break down the laboratory door. One more time they call
out to Jekyll before taking this last desperate move.

"Jekyll," called Utterson, "I demand to see you." But there was
no reply. Then: "Utterson!" said a voice, "for God's sake, have
mercy!" "Ah, that's not Jekyll's voice—it's Hyde's!" cried Utterson, and with that the two men break down the door.

Suddenly Utterson and Poole stand inside the laboratory. All is
still. Then they see the body of a man, still twitching, who has
clearly just destroyed himself with poison. It is the body of Edward Hyde, dressed in clothes far too large for him, such as might
have fit Dr. Jekyll. They rummage further through the disordered
laboratory looking for Jekyll's body, but find nothing. A pious
book lies on a table, one known to have been prized by the good
doctor, but with startling blasphemies written on the margins.
Finally they do locate a laboratory glass, which obviously has
been used many times, the sight of which somehow strikes them
with horror. At last they come across three envelopes. The first
contains a will, drawn up by Henry Jekyll, leaving all his posses-
sions to Gabriel John Utterson. The second is a brief note in the
doctor's hand instructing Utterson to read the letter left him by
Dr. Lanyon. The third is a "considerable packet sealed in several
places." Utterson decides to call the police, but first he reads Dr.
Lanyon's letter.

Dr. Lanyon's Narrative

Four days ago, Lanyon had written to Utterson, he had received a letter from Henry Jekyll, a letter urging him most strongly to postpone all other engagements he might have for tonight, go to Jekyll's house, force open the door to Jekyll's cabinet in his laboratory (Poole having orders to allow Lanyon to do this), and remove all contents and return with them to his home. Then Lanyon is to be alone at midnight in his home and is to admit into his house the person who will present himself in Jekyll's name, and to give this man the contents withdrawn from the cabinet.

Lanyon goes on to relate that he decided to do as he was asked, that he went to Jekyll's laboratory and did remove from the cabinet what appeared to be "a simple crystalline salt of a white colour." At midnight a knock came at his door and Lanyon tells how he found "a small man crouching against the pillars of the portico," a man dressed in clothes outlandishly large for him, who would have been laughable had he not been so revolting. Impatiently the man, who is Hyde, of course, demands the crystalline salts, and "At sight of the contents, he uttered one loud sob of such immense relief that I sat petrified."

The small, revolting man then consumed the drug and began to undergo profound and horrible changes until, there before Lanyon's eyes, stood Henry Jekyll. Lanyon concluded his letter: "What he told me in the next hour, I cannot bring my mind to set on paper. I saw what I saw, I heard what I heard, and my soul sickened at it; and yet now when that sight has faded from my eyes, I ask myself if I believe it, and I cannot answer. My life is shaken to its roots; sleep has left me; the deadliest terror sits by me at all hours of the day and night; I feel that my days are numbered, and that I must die; and yet I shall die incredulous." Next the stunned Utterson read the largish packet which proved to be

Henry Jekyll's Full Statement of the Case

Jekyll's account can be summarized as follows: He began with a description of himself and his life. He was, he writes, born to a large fortune, "fond of the respect of the wise and good among my fellowmen, and thus, as might have been supposed, with every guarantee of an honourable and distinguished future." The worst of his faults, Jekyll noted of himself, "was a certain impatient gaiety of disposition" which seemed harmless enough but which he "found hard to reconcile with my imperious desire to carry my head high, and wear a more than commonly grave countenance before the public." "Hence," he continued, "it came about that I concealed my pleasure; and that when I reached years of reflection, and began to look round me and take stock of my progress and position in the world, I stood already committed to a profound duplicity of life." He goes on to relate how he was guilty of certain irregularities of life which he regarded with a "morbid sense of shame." He had, he noted, a "dual nature," moreover, "both sides of me were in dead earnest; I was no more myself when I laid aside restraint and plunged in shame, than when I laboured, in the eye of day, at the furtherance of knowledge or the relief of sorrow and suffering." From all of this Jekyll concluded, "that man is not truly one, but truly two." He even hazarded the conjecture that man would eventually be "known for a mere polity of multifarious, incongruous, and independent denizens." In this way he came to recognize "the thorough and primitive duality of man."

At this point, Jekyll says, he began to dwell "on the thought of the separation of these elements. If each . . . . could but be housed in separate identities, life would be relieved of all that was unbearable." At this point he began to experiment and eventually produced a drug that could accomplish just such a separation of his two personalities, buying from a certain chemist the last special ingredient necessary to make him transformative compound. Jekyll then took the drug and began to undergo profound changes: "I felt younger, lighter, happier in body; within I was conscious of a heady recklessness, a current of disordered sensual images running like a mill race in my fancy, a solution of the bonds of obligation, an unknown but not an innocent freedom of the soul. I knew myself, at the first breath of this new life, to be more wicked, tenfold more wicked, sold a slave to my original evil; and the thought, in that moment, braced and delighted me like wine." He then looked in the mirror and saw that person with whom we have already become familiar: the small, young, somehow deformed body of Edward Hyde.

"This, too," Jekyll reasoned, "was myself." And so Jekyll welcomed Hyde, and concluded, "all human beings . . . are commingled out of good and evil; and Edward Hyde, alone in the ranks of mankind, was pure evil." Now Jekyll found that he had but to quaff the drug and he was transformed into Hyde, and could then indulge in all those pleasures which hitherto he either had forbade himself, or had indulged in only with guilt and anxiety that he might be discovered. To make it even easier, he took the apartment in Soho where, as Hyde, he could live as he pleased, and he also drew up the will to which Utterson had so greatly objected. At first the pleasures he pursued were simply "undignified," but, in Hyde's hands, they soon began to "turn towards the monstrous." But Jekyll felt no guilt, for it "was Hyde, after all, and Hyde alone that was guilty. Jekyll was no worse; he woke again to his good qualities seemingly unimpaired; he would even make haste, where it was possible, to undo the evil done by Hyde. And thus conscience slumbered."

So everything proceeded for a while as Jekyll had planned until one dark day he found that he had turned into Hyde even without taking the drug! "Yes, I had gone to bed Henry Jekyll; I had awakened Edward Hyde." Jekyll was terrified. How could he return to his normal shape and personality? He found the answer by taking the drug which this time reversed him from Hyde to Jekyll again.

Because of this frightening experience Jekyll felt he now had to choose between his two personalities. It was a hard choice, but at last he determined to remain as Jekyll, though he did not give up the house in Soho, nor destroy the clothes of Edward Hyde which he kept in his cabinet. For two months he led a life of great severity, until at length he "began to be tortured with throes and longings, as of Hyde struggling after freedom; and at last, in an hour of moral weakness, I once again compounded and swallowed the transforming draught."

It was at this time that Hyde killed Dr. Carew. "Instantly the spirit of hell awoke in me and raged. With a transport of glee, I mauled the unresisting body, tasting delight from every blow; and it was not till weariness had begun to succeed, that I was suddenly, in the top fit of my delerium, struck through the heart by a cold thrill of terror." Then, when Hyde took the draught, and his usual personality reemerged, Jekyll wrote that "Henry Jekyll, with streaming tears of gratitude and remorse, had fallen upon his knees and lifted his clasped hands to God."

Henceforth, Jekyll realized, he could no longer be Hyde, for Hyde was now a wanted man. He now must confine himself to "the better part of my existence." So Jekyll once again lived a life dedicated to the good, until one day, as he sat in the park reflecting that he was, after all, "like my neighbours; ... comparing myself with other men, comparing my active good–will with the lazy cruelty of their neglect," he suddenly was transformed into Hyde! Now his situation was desperate. He must not be seen in public, yet if he returned home in the form of Hyde his own servants would turn him in. It was at this point that he wrote the letter to Lanyon, and, with the doctor's help, recovered the drug and became again his Jekyll self.

Jekyll now lived in horror of his other self but found that he could not avoid unwilling transformations into Hyde even without the drug. So he was consigned to a life of confinement in his laboratory where he could get at the drug when this happened, but he also discovered that more and more of the drug was required to bring him from the form of Hyde back into the form of Jekyll. "The powers of Hyde," he noted, "seemed to have grown with the sickliness of Jekyll." And then—he began to run out of the drug!

He was now, of course, confined to the laboratory, and slipped frequently into the form of Edward Hyde. It was in this form that Poole once saw him outside the laboratory door with his face masked. Desperately he sent Poole out repeatedly to ransack London for the correct ingredient with which to make a new supply of the drug, but always it failed to work. Only gradually did he realize that "my first supply was impure, and that it was that unknown impurity which lent efficacy to the draught." Jekyll concluded his letter (and with this Stevenson also concludes the story):

> About a week has passed, and I am now finishing this statement under the influence of the last of the old powders. This, then, is the last time, short of a miracle, that Henry Jekyll can think his own thoughts or see his own face (now how sadly altered!) in the glass. Nor must I delay too long to bring my

writing to an end; for if my narrative has hitherto escaped destruction, it has been by a combination of great prudence and great good luck. Should the throes of change take me in the act of writing it, Hyde will tear it in pieces; but if some time shall have elapsed after I have laid it by, his wonderful selfishness and circumscription to the moment will probably save it once again from the action of his apelike spite. And indeed the doom that is closing on us both, has already changed and crushed him. Half an hour from now, when I shall again and forever reindue that hated personality, I know how I shall sit shuddering and weeping in my chair, or continue, with the most strained and fearstruck ecstasy of listening, to pace up and down this room (my last earthly refuge) and give ear to every sound of menace. Will Hyde die upon the scaffold? or will he find courage to release himself at the last moment? God knows; I am careless; this is my true hour of death, and what is to follow concerns another than myself. Here then, as I lay down the pen and proceed to seal up my confession, I bring the life of that unhappy Henry Jekyll to an end.

*　　*　　*　　*　　*

We can begin by contrasting the description of Henry Jekyll with that of Edward Hyde. We are told that Jekyll was a "large, well–made, smooth–faced man of fifty, with something of a slyish cast perhaps, but every mark of capacity and kindness." So there is no reason to suppose that Jekyll did not have many good qualities. Only the hint of a "slyish cast" betrays the fact that hidden underneath the goodness of Henry Jekyll there was a person of more doubtful character. Later Jekyll describes himself in more detail as a man "fond of the respect of the wise and good among my fellow-men." This tells us that in addition to his natural store of goodness and kindness Henry Jekyll had a desire for approbation by his fellows and so struck a certain pose in front of mankind, that is, adopted a pleasing persona that would bring him the approval and respect of others.

Jekyll noted another side to his personality, however, which was at variance with this persona: "a certain impatient gaiety of disposition." This led him to seek certain pleasures in life which he found hard to reconcile with his "imperious desire" to carry his head high. Hence, Jekyll noted, he adopted a "more than commonly grave countenance before the public." In other words, the grave countenance Jekyll publicly struck was a mask to shield from others another side to his personality that Jekyll did not want anyone to see and which he regarded with "a morbid sense of shame." As a consequence, Jekyll wrote, "I concealed my pleasures" and "stood already committed to a profound duplicity of life."

Jekyll displayed psychological insight. He was aware of the duality of his own nature, and declared that "man is not truly one, but truly two." He could even hazard the conjecture that man is made up of a whole assortment of partselves, that his personality is not single, but is like a village of people, an insight modern depth psychology corroborates. He saw this duality as "thorough" and "primitive," that is, archetypal and therefore present from the beginning as a fundamental aspect of man's basic psychological structure. Armed with this kind of psychological insight into himself, Jekyll might have gone on to great heights of conscious development but failed to do so because of a fundamental psychological error, as we shall see.

Hyde is described as young, full of hellish energy, small, and somehow deformed. He is a "Juggernaut," "not like a man," a person who evoked hatred in others at the very sight of him. He has a black, sneering coldness, and is incapable of human feeling, and therefore is without any twinge of conscience and so is incapable of guilt. Hyde's youthfulness suggests that as the shadow personality of Jekyll, he contains unused energy. The Shadow, as we have seen, includes the unlived life, and to touch upon the shadow personality is to receive an infusion of new, that is, youthful energy. Hyde's small size and deformed appearance indicates that as the shadow personality Hyde has not lived very much in Jekyll's outer life. Having dwelt for the most part in the darkness of the unconscious he is deformed in appearance, like a tree forced to grow among the rocks and in the shadow of other trees. Hyde's lack of conscience, described by Jekyll as a "solution of the bonds of obligation," is also characteristic of the shadow personality. It is as though the Shadow leaves moral feelings and obligations up to the ego personality while he or she strives to live out of inner and forbidden impulses quite devoid of the mitigating effects of a sense of right or wrong.

But perhaps the most important thing we are told about Edward Hyde comes from Jekyll's comment that when he first was transformed by the drug into Hyde "I knew myself . . . to be more wicked, tenfold more wicked, sold a slave to my original evil . . . " At first Jekyll has only seen in himself a certain "gaiety of disposition," a pleasure–seeking side that might have led to mischief but nothing more, but once he has become Hyde he realizes he is far more evil than he ever supposed. From this description it appears that the shadow personality begins with our personal dark side, but at some point contacts a deeper, more archetypal level of evil which is so strong that Jekyll could say of Hyde that he alone among men was pure evil. In the hands of this archetypal evil the pleasure–seeking mischief in which Jekyll wanted to engage soon led to truly satanic activity, as exemplified in the hellish murder of Dr. Carew, which was done for the pure joy of evil and destruction. We can see this same satanic quality emerging in those situations in which a person cold–bloodedly kills others, either in war or crime, without evident remorse. It is an archetypal evil that both shocks and fascinates us and draws us with horrified absorption to the daily reading of our newspapers.

C. G. Jung once wrote that we become what we do. This helps us understand even more the reason for Jekyll's demise. Once he decides to *be* Hyde, even if only for a while, he tends to *become* Hyde. The deliberate decision to *do* evil leads to our becoming evil. This is why living out the darkest implses of the Shadow cannot be a solution to the shadow problem, for we can easily become possessed by or absorbed into evil if we try such a thing. This attests to the archetypal nature of evil, for it is one of the qualities of the archetypes that they can possess the ego, which is like being devoured by or made identical with the archetype.

Jekyll himself becomes aware of this danger after he finds himself involuntarily turning into Hyde. This was an enormous shock to him. He had expected to be able to move from Jekyll to Hyde and back again at will, but now he finds that Hyde is taking over. His former confidence, which led him to say, "the moment I choose, I can be rid of Mr. Hyde," is now gone. This attitude shows a carelessness toward evil that predisposed Jekyll toward possession. It comes up again in the story in the scene in which Jekyll sits in the park and reflects that he is, after all, "like my neighbours," and compares himself favorably with other men, noting his active good will in contrast to the "lazy neglect" of others. Jekyll's careless disregard for the powers of evil, together with his desire to escape the tension of his dual nature, paves the way for his ultimate destruction.

So at this point in the story Jekyll resolves to have nothing more to do with the Hyde part of his personality and even declares to Utterson, "I swear to God, I swear to God I will never set eyes on him again. I bind my honour to you that I am done with him in this world. It is all at an end." And Jekyll does try to have done with Hyde. He renews his old life, becomes more dedicated than ever to doing good works, and also, for the first time, becomes devoted to religion as well.

We must assume that Jekyll's devotion to religion means that he went through formal religious observances, perhaps joining a Church of some kind. We know, of course, that Jekyll's religion is not sincere. He knows nothing of God, but is hoping to find in formalized religion and in his own religious pretensions a defense against being overcome by Hyde. No doubt many of us today are using religion in this way, especially those religious creeds that decry man's sins, threaten the sinful man with punishment, and encourage good deeds as the sign of salvation. This kind of religion tends to draw as members those persons who are consciously or unconsciously struggling to hold in check their shadow personalities.

But the attempt does not work with Dr. Jekyll, and Hyde has now grown stronger within him. Hyde as the shadow personality continues to exist in the unconscious and is now, more than ever, struggling to be free, that is, to possess Jekyll's personality so he can live as he wants to. The dark side has been strengthened too much, and the attempt to hold him in check and keep him locked in the basement of the psyche fails because Hyde is now stronger than Jekyll. So Stevenson is telling us that if living out the Shadow is not the answer, neither is the repression of the Shadow the answer, for both leave the personality split into two.

There is also Jekyll's insincerity and religious pretension. Both his religion and his desire to have nothing to do any longer with Hyde stem from his desire for self–preservation and not from his moral feelings. It is not for spiritual reasons, but because he fears destruction, that Jekyll wants Hyde contained. Underneath there still exists his unrecognized longing for evil, as is evidenced by the fact that even in the midst of this great resolve to have nothing to do with Hyde he did not destroy Hyde's clothes or give up the apartment in Soho. We could say that at this point the only way Jekyll could have kept from being overcome by evil was if his soul were filled with a spirit more powerful than that of evil; but in allowing himself to become Hyde, Jekyll emptied his soul and evil could take possession of him.

Henry Jekyll's fundamental mistake was his desire to escape the tension of the opposites within him. As we have seen, he was gifted with a modicum of psychological consciousness, more than most men, for he knew that he had a dual nature; he was aware that there was another one in him whose desires were counter to his more usual desires for the approbation of mankind. Had he enlarged this consciousness and carried the tension of the opposites within him, it would have led to the development of his personality; in the language we have been using, he would have individuated. But Jekyll chose instead to try to escape this tension by means of the transforming drug, so that he could be both Jekyll and Hyde and have the pleasures and benefits of living out both sides of his personality without guilt or tension. For as Jekyll, it is worth noting, he felt no responsibility for Hyde. "For it was Hyde, after all, and Hyde alone that was guilty," he once declared.

This gives us a clue to how the problem of the Shadow can be met. What was Jekyll's failure may tell us where to go if the conclusion of our drama with the Shadow is to be successful: success may lie in carrying that tension which Jekyll refused. Both repression of the knowledge of the Shadow, and identification with the Shadow, are attempts to escape the tension of the opposites within ourselves, attempts to "loose the bonds" that hold together within us a light and dark side. The motive, of course, is to escape the pain of the problem, but if escaping the pain leads to psychological disaster, carrying the pain may give the possibility for wholeness.

Carrying such a tension of the opposites is like a Crucifixion. We must be as one suspended between the opposites, a painful state to bear. But in such a state of suspension the grace of God is able to operate within us. The problem of our duality can never be resolved on the level of the ego; it permits no rational solution.

But where there is consciousness of a problem, the Self, the *Imago Dei* within us can operate and bring about an irrational synthesis of the personality.

To put it another way, if we consciously carry the burden of the opposites in our nature, the secret, irrational, healing processes that go on in us unconsciously can operate to our benefit, and work toward the synthesis of the personality. This irrational, healing process, which finds a way around seemingly insurmountable obstacles, has a particularly feminine quality to it. It is the rational, logical masculine mind that declares that opposites like ego and Shadow, light and dark, can never be united. However, the feminine spirit is capable of finding a synthesis where logic says none can be found. For this reason it is worth noting that in Stevenson's story the feminine figures are few and far between and when they do occur they are seen in an exclusively negative light. There is not one major character in the book who is a woman. Jekyll, Enfield, Utterson, Poole, the handwriting expert Mr. Guest, Dr. Lanyon—all are men. The women figures have only brief mention. There is the woman who cared for Hyde's apartment, an "evil–faced" woman, cold and witchlike. There is a brief mention of the frightened maid whom Utterson meets when he goes to Jekyll's house on the final night, who is described as "hysterically whimpering." There is, of course, also the little girl who was trampled on, and the women who grouped around Hyde who were "wild as harpies." Even Hyde, in the laboratory that final night, is described as "weeping like a woman or a lost soul." The only vaguely positive allusion to a woman or to the feminine is the maid who witnessed the murder of Dr. Carew, but even she is said to have fainted at the sight.

In short, the feminine comes off badly in Stevenson's story. It is cold and witchlike, weak and ineffective, or is victimized, which suggests that the feminine spirit was rendered inoperative, and was unable to help in the situation. Translated into psychological language, we can say that when psychological consciousness is refused, as Jekyll had refused it, the feminine part of us, our very souls, weakens and languishes and falls into despair, a tragedy, for it is this very feminine power that can help find a way around what is otherwise an insoluble problem.

A comment on Mr. Utterson is in order. The portrayal of Utterson is a testimony to the skill of Stevenson as a storyteller, for while the majority of the narrative is told to us through his eyes and experiences, he himself never intrudes into the spotlight. His character is adroitly drawn. We like Utterson, we can picture him in our minds, we can follow his thoughts and feelings and reactions, yet the spotlight of the story always shines through him onto the central mystery of Jekyll and Hyde so that Utterson never takes over the center of the stage. Because of this we may be inclined simply to dismiss Utterson as a literary device, a necessary figure to have so that the story may be told, but not a character who is likely to have anything to teach us about the mystery of good and evil.

But in fact Utterson is more important than he seems, for he is the human figure whose sensibilities are aroused by evil and in whose consciousness the full story of good and evil, ego and Shadow, finally emerges. He represents the human being who has a sufficiently strong feeling function that he is shocked by evil and can therefore resist being overcome by it. It is exactly this feeling function, which enables a human being to react with horror at the depths of evil, that was weak in Jekyll and totally lacking in Hyde.

It is also necessary that evil eventually be known by someone. The doings of Jekyll and Hyde were a secret, but secrets have a way of trying to emerge. Every secret is propelled by hidden inner forces toward human consciousness, and for this reason evil deeds eventually emerge into the awareness of humanity in general, or someone in particular. Notice, for instance, that early in the story Utterson's mind is tortured by what he does not know, and he is unable to sleep. This is a sure sign that the unconscious is troubling Utterson, and is seeking to find a way to bring into his consciousness the dreadful and dark secret life of Jekyll and Hyde. So in the story it is Utterson whose consciousness becomes the container for the knowledge of evil, and thus he represents the ego at its most human and best, a kind of redemptive person whose dawning awareness of what is happening, and horrified feelings, provide a human safeguard against the takeover of human life by the powers of darkness.

But how about Dr. Lanyon? He too came to see the nature of evil, but in the wrong way. Lanyon had not sought out the mystery of Jekyll and Hyde as did Utterson, and when the full extent of the evil broke in on him, it was too much for him. He saw evil too quickly, and looked into it too deeply, without the necessary preparation or the necessary human support. And that is the other side of becoming conscious of evil. We must become aware of it, but to look into it too deeply and naively may give us a shock from which we cannot recover.

The demonic drug that Jekyll concocted to achieve his transformation into Hyde is also worth a comment, especially in this present time of history when we are surrounded on all sides by drugs with mind–altering effects. I have often noted that, in some instances at least, alcohol seems to change people from a Jekyll to a Hyde personality. A person is one way until he or she takes a few drinks and then out comes the ugly side of the personality. In certain cases it may well be that at the bottom of the urge to drink is the struggle of the Shadow to assert itself, just as in our story Hyde yearned for Jekyll to take the drug so he could live out his own dark life.

We can also note that although the evil part of Jekyll's personality destroyed him, it also eventually destroyed itself. No sooner was Jekyll completely possessed by Hyde than Hyde himself died by suicide. This too is instructive, for it tells us that evil eventually overreaches itself and brings about its own destruction. Evidently evil cannot live on his own, but can exist only when there is something good upon which it can feed, a point we will look at more closely in Chapter Nine.

Finally, this is an appropriate place to make a few comments on how we can deal with evil. When evil manifests itself there is a tendency to want to oppose it directly. Sometimes we must do this, but there is danger in this direct opposition to evil because of the tendency, as Laurens van der Post once put it, to become like the evil that we oppose. An example of this would be American behaviour in the Vietnam war. America entered the war, ostensibly at least, to oppose the evil of the Viet Cong and North Vietnamese communists, who were assassinating village chieftans and committing other atrocities. Yet by the time the war was over we had become guilty of atrocities as bad as any of those committed by the communists. For evil is contagious. One can hardly come near it without being affected or contaminated by it, and this makes dealing with it a problem.

Yet sometimes unless evil is opposed it simply becomes larger and stronger than ever. The worst thing to do with evil is to appease it. When Chamberlain's England sought to appease the evil of Hitler's Germany, it simply increased the evil in the situation. Even on the level of family life this is true. To appease a troublesome, demanding child is simply to feed and strengthen those negative qualities in the child. Similarly, a man or woman who seeks to placate demanding weaknesses in his or her spouse only makes these evil tendencies all the greater.

I am indebted to Marie–Louise von Franz for a number of these insights into dealing with evil in her *Shadow and Evil in Fairy Tales*.[4] She points out that in fairy tales there is no one way of dealing with evil. First one deals with evil one way, then another way, depending on the individual circumstances. Sometimes we must resolutely oppose evil; sometimes we must approach it indirectly. Usually we need to meet evil with a firmness and consciousness, but at other times we may even need, at least for the moment, to look the other way. Always, however, we need to know what we are doing, as though evil can only be overcome by a superior consciousness.

The story of Jekyll and Hyde tells us that evil is fascinating; this is a quality of evil that we have already noted. Because of its fascination evil has considerable power over the human soul, so much power, in fact, that C. G. Jung once aptly commented that only two things could keep a person's soul from falling under the power of evil: if a person's soul is filled with a power greater than the power of evil, or if a person is contained in a warm, related human community. Jung once wrote to William W., a founder of Alcoholics Anonymous, "I am strongly convinced that the evil principle prevailing in this world leads the unrecognized spiritual need into perdition, if it is not counteracted either by real religious insight or by the protective wall of human community. An ordinary man, not protected by an action from above and isolated in society, cannot resist the power of evil."[5]

Jung mentioned the dangers of isolation. This danger cannot be stressed too much. The coldblooded killers of our time, for instance, are emotionally isolated people. Conversely, those who have been bonded to others through eros have a modicum of protection against the worst danger of cold evil. For this reason early childhood conditioning is extremely important. To have been bonded by love to one's parents or surrogate parents lends to a soul a warmth of human feeling that is the ultimate defense against evil. On the other hand, where this bonding has not occurred the dangers of succumbing to evil, either as its victim or perpetrator, are far greater.

The story of Jekyll and Hyde tells us that possession is the worst form of evil. Jekyll's soul became possessed by Hyde and with this came his destruction. Possession by evil is more likely to occur when the powers of evil are not taken sufficiently seriously. Von Franz points out the dangers of *frevel*. *Frevel* is a German word denoting a careless attitude. We derive the English word "frivolous" from it. For example, persons who carelessly take drugs without due regard for the potential dangers of their experience are exercising *frevel*. But there are many ways to exhibit a careless disregard of the powers of evil, and wherever this occurs the danger from evil increases.

The poet William Blake once said, "Form comes from heaven, but energy from hell." It might be said that the task of life is to unite these two opposites. That is one reason the Shadow is so fascinating to us, for the Shadow, as we saw in the story, contains a lot of energy, and energy exerts a compelling fascination on us. But we cannot get into the life of the Shadow heedlessly, as we have seen, nor is reason of much help. The Shadow cannot be denied, but must be dealt with in the light of a higher authority. The religions of the world have recognized this and instructed mankind in the art of living in the consciousness of God. However, for many persons today the traditional ways of mediating the consciousness of God are no longer efficacious, and some persons now turn to psychology in order to relate directly to the God within, which psychology calls the Self. In the process our dreams are of great importance and infallibly inform us, among other things, when our souls are in danger. One can understand why the American Indians said that the Great Spirit sent mankind dreams so that we would not wander in darkness and fall under the power of evil.

Notes

[1] *Time,* May 7, 1979, p. 26.

[2] Robert Louis Stevenson, Vol. IX, *Across the Plains* (New York, N.Y.: The Davos Press, 1906). Also see his other novels, *The Master of Ballantrae* and *The Weir of Hermiston,* which deal with much the same theme.

[3] Barbara Hannah, *Striving Towards Wholeness* (New York, N.Y.: G. P. Putnam's Sons, 1971).

[4] Marie–Louise von Franz, *Shadow and Evil in Fairy Tales* (Zurich, Switzerland: Spring Publications, 1974).

[5] C. G. Jung, *Letters 2* (Princeton, New Jersey: Princeton University Press, 1975), p. 624.

CHAPTER EIGHT

The Devil in Post-Biblical Mythology and Folklore

We have already seen how the devil fared in the Old and New Testaments. Now it is time to see the role the devil has played in mythology and folklore of the post–biblical era.

One of the many names for the devil is Lucifer. It is a curious name for him because it means "the light–bringer," and we ordinarily associate the devil with the powers of darkness.

The name is derived from the biblical verses, and the uses made of these verses by the early Church Fathers. In Isaiah 14:12–15 we read:

> *How did you come to fall from the heavens,*
> *Daystar, son of Dawn?*
> *How did you come to be thrown to the ground,*
> *you who enslaved the nations?*
> *You who used to think to yourself,*
> *"I will climb up to the heavens;*
> *and higher than the stars of God*
> *I will set my throne.*
> *I will sit on the Mount of Assembly*
> *in the recesses of the north,*
> *I will climb to the top of thunderclouds,*
> *I will rival the Most High."*
> *What! Now you have fallen to Sheol*
> *to the very bottom of the abyss!*

No doubt these verses were originally meant to refer to Babylon, the great city that had conquered the near East, but had in turn been defeated and cast down. The Fathers of the Church, however, took these verses as symbolizing Satan and his downfall from on high with God and around them built up an elaborate legend of the angel Lucifer, his original home with God, his pretensions to power, and his ultimate fall from heaven to earth. They were supported in this endeavor by another biblical verse, Luke 10:18, in which Jesus says to the seventy–two disciples who are returning triumphantly from their mission of teaching and healing: "I watched Satan fall like lightning from Heaven."

According to the Fathers of the Church, Satan originally dwelt with God as one of His principal angels, and his original name was Lucifer, lightbringer, translated in the Jerusalem Bible, Isaiah 14:12, as "Daystar." But Lucifer fell prey to the sins of pride, conceit, and ambition; he was not content to be one of God's angels, but wanted to usurp the Heavenly power. Indeed, some say that he actually had the audacity to try to sit upon the throne of God.

For this affrontery, the Archangel Michael took up arms against Lucifer and drove him from heaven. Lucifer fell to earth, where he took up his abode in hell, and exerted his domination over the world. From this vantage point the fallen angel sought to make the souls of mankind part of his kingdom and to rule the earth as he once tried to rule heaven. "In this manner, then," says Origen, "did that being once exist as light before he went astray, and fell to this place, and had his glory turned into dust." [1] And Archelaus, an early Bishop of the Church, writes, "Hence also certain of the angels, refusing to submit themselves to the commandment of God, resisted His will; and one of them indeed fell like a flash of lightning upon the earth, . . . And that angel who was cast down to earth, finding no further admittance into any of the regions of heaven, now flaunts about among men, deceiving them, and luring them to become transgressors like himself, and even to this day he is an adversary to the commandments of God." [2]

It is not hard to see parallels between this Christian mythology and Zoroastrian thinking, Ahura–Mazda being represented by the Archangel Michael and Ahriman by Satan or Lucifer. It is also reflected in the Gospel of St. John, where the devil is repeatedly called "the prince of this world," and the earth is generally represented as under his power, while Christ descends from above to win souls away from his influence. So Jesus says to his disciples, in anticipation of his Crucifixion, "I shall not talk with you any longer, because the prince of this world is on his way." [3]

The legend of Lucifer was also shared by Jewish thinkers, and the Talmud has an interesting variation of the story. In the Talmudic version the downfall of Lucifer came because he was jealous of man. When Adam was created, so the Rabbis taught, all the angels had to bow down before the new king of the earth, but Satan was jealous and refused to do so and was therefore cast out of heaven.

Along with Satan there went a host of demons and lesser devils; it was believed that evil thoughts that come into the minds and hearts of mankind were inspired by this demonic host. As we have already seen, it was these many dark powers that the people of the New Testament era supposed caused disease, inspired mankind to sin, and brought about mental afflictions. The last theologian known to have actually calculated the number of the demons of Satan is the theologian of Basel, Martinus Barrhause. According to his calculations the exact number was 2,665,866,746,664— two trillian, six hundred and sixty–five billion, eight hundred and sixty–six million, seven hundred and forty–six thousand, six hundred and sixty–four.[4] With such a vast army at the devil's disposal it is no wonder mankind is plagued by so many misfortunes.

This legend of Lucifer explains very nicely how evil came into the world of mankind; however, it does not explain why God let it happen. It seems unfair that God's unruly angel, who was found unfit for heaven, should be sent to the earth to plague mankind. What had mankind done to deserve the fate of having to house such an unwelcome exile? One might think that God would have been more noble in dealing with the problems of His own household rather than foisting them off on helpless humanity.

In spite of this deficiency in the legend of Lucifer, however, it remains an instructive story. From the vantage point of psychology the story describes an archetype, that is, a typical and inevitable part of the human psyche and the way it functions. Looked at from this point of view, the legend describes a fateful split in the human psyche, so that a psyche that was originally whole became divided against itself. The split in heaven thus corresponds to a split in man's psyche, and this split, as we have already seen, is exacerbated in Christian consciousness by the difficulty we have in dealing with the Shadow. According to this story, it would seem that a devil has truly gotten into the psyche of Western man; that an archetypal evil of dark power stirs up our consciousness, promotes difficulties, and brings about destruction.

The legend makes it clear that we dare not be too sanguine about mankind nor too naive about solutions to the problem of evil. For instance, if evil is an archetypal power in the human psyche, as our legend suggests, then not even the best possible environments for people to grow up in and live in will keep evil out of the picture. It can even be suggested that incorrigible criminal personalities are a living representation of this archetypal power. Nor can we assume that all evil behaviour in mankind would disappear if every child received the right kind of parenting, with plenty of love and affection. While no doubt this would help, the fact is that many children do *not* receive this kind of parenting, and the fact that they do not, but are surrounded by dark forces, attests to the power of the archetype to disrupt human life. And even in the child blessed by a positive parental upbringing there is always the possibility for a fatal twist toward evil to take place. Such is the power of the archetype.

The legend also tells us what is at the core of the archetype of evil: the power drive. Lucifer's sin was in trying to replace God on the heavenly throne. It was the desire for power that brought about his downfall and led to mankind's plight. On the psychological level, this destructive power drive can be seen as an archetypal quality of the human ego that wants to set itself up in place of the Self. It is the dark tendency built into our ego structure that tries to establish the ego's domination over the whole psyche, rather than allowing the God–given Center of the psyche to rule. From this perspective, human egocentricity is at the core of the problem of moral evil, hence the great efforts of religions such as Christianity to overcome this power drive in man and help him to relate humbly and properly to God as his Center.

Significantly, the first thing that happened to Jesus after he received the Holy Spirit from God following his baptism was his encounter with Satan in the wilderness, a Satan who is clearly a personification of the power drive, for he says to Jesus: "If you are the Son of God, tell these stones to turn into loaves." And, "If you are the Son of God, throw yourself down." And finally, after showing Jesus all the kingdoms of the world, "I will give you all these, if you fall at my feet and worship me." [5]

From the modern point of view, the legend of Lucifer may seem naive and fanciful, but we should not overlook its wisdom. It is because the legend of Lucifer deals with an archetype that the legend was devised in the first place. We can say that the human mind is compelled to devise such stories in order to express and relate to its own archetypal foundations. Today we no longer fashion and follow legends such as this, but the myth–making mind, stripped of its proper function, produces distorted myths. That is, the "devil" is now seen in others, and the mythological picture of God and Satan struggling against each other is projected out into world politics with Russians playing the adversary role for Americans and vice versa. It would be better to have our divine myths back than to fall into the paranoid states of mind that a mythology projected onto other people produces.

In popular folklore the devil has many forms and shapes. In the New Testament, for instance, we read that the devil can transform himself into an angel of light, for St. Paul tells us that ". . . Satan himself goes disguised as an angel of light." [6] He can also appear in human form, as in the *Faust* story in which the devil, or one of his servants, appears as Mephistopheles and acts like a cynical, clever, perceptive man. He can appear in an exceedingly ugly form, as a person embodying all hated and repugnant human qualities, but at the same time he can appear in an exceedingly beautiful form, as an extremely attractive man, or even as a beautiful and seductive woman. It was in this form that he tried to seduce the pious St. Augustine, or so the Saint believed. In animal form the devil typically appears as a roaring lion, a ferocious dragon, a serpent, a wolf, or a black dog. His consort animals include bats, rats, mice, vermin, and flies.

Among the devil's human identities one of the most important is his propensity to appear as a priest. It has been said that he likes nothing better than to put on priestly robes and, if possible, occupy a pulpit. But, according to the legend, his true identity is always betrayed by his limp, said to be the result of his fall from heaven.

The devil also has many colors. Black is one of his favorite colors, but he also uses red and blue. The expression "the blues" is said to come from the association of the color blue with the devil.

The ape is another of the theriomorphic representations of the devil. In fact, he is sometimes called "the ape of God" because of the way he apes the Deity. The early Christians saw the close comparison between many of the Greek myths and certain Christian stories, such as the parallel between the story of Asklepius, god of healing, and Christ. The early Christians said that this affinity was the work of the devil, who tried to draw people away from the true worship of God to the false worship of pagan deities by devising pagan tales closely resembling the Christian ones.

This mercurial aspect of the devil betrays his close identification with the unconscious, which is also mercurial in nature, being first one thing and then another, assuming first one symbolic form and then another. The unconscious does indeed have this devilish quality. It contains, as we have seen, the disagreeable qualities of our nature that we have rejected from consciousness. It refuses to be absorbed into a monolithic conscious standpoint and constantly favors paradox over a clear-cut expression of truth. It is also a trickster, for the unconscious is full of tricks that have the ultimate effect of tricking us into further consciousness but seem at the time to be like the devil himself. Of course this is only one aspect of the unconscious. The unconscious also has its deeply moral aspect and represents an ultimate truth from which we can never escape, but the devilish side is there too and for this reason the unconscious is viewed suspiciously. It can easily be seen as the devil by those who are afraid of paradox and who need the security of what is supposed to be an absolute and inflexible truth.

But perhaps the most psychologically revealing aspect of the devil in post-biblical mythology is the way he is connected with the attributes of repressed pagan deities. The devil, for instance, is often represented in goat form because pagan deities of the woods appeared in goat's form. His cloven hoof can be seen to be Pan's hoof come back again, and his horns are said to come from Dionysus. However, it is also said that the horns of the devil come from the horned god worshiped in the nature religion of old England known as Wicca.

In the old nature religion of England there were two deities: a beneficent female goddess of healing and fertility, and a beneficent male god who was horned. For about a thousand years after the arrival of Christianity in England the Church tolerated the old religion, perhaps because the Church did not feel strong enough to move against it. But eventually a movement developed to repress the old religion and this culminated in a bull against it issued in 1484 by Pope Innocent VIII. From this time on Wicca was forced underground, and it was after this that witches on brooms with black cats began to appear in English folklore and imagery—the old nature goddess coming back in a sinister form because she had been rejected. And it was after this that it became popular to represent the devil as horned, the old horned god coming back as the devil because he was now the object of repression. In this way truly "The gods of the old religion always become the devils of the new." [7]

This indicates that the figure of the devil is a representation or personification of those aspects of the human psyche that have been repressed, and consequently, banished to the unconscious. Christianity was able to absorb many of the roles and functions of the ancient pagan deities, but not all. For instance, the function of Zeus, father–god and ultimate authority over all the other gods of ancient Greece, was absorbed into the Christian image of God the Father. And Apollo, inspirer of reason, harmony, and order, was absorbed into the Christian reliance upon reason and its civilizing capacity. Asklepius, too, was integrated into Christianity, as his functions of healing were taken over by Christ, who was himself a healer, or the saints, who continued to have a healing influence on needy mankind. But other deities found no representation in the Christian spirit. Dionysus, for instance, god of ecstasy, of abandonment to the powers of nature and instinct, and of uninhibited joyfulness, found no home in the Christian spirit. Nor did Pan, the deity who wandered in the woods and expressed the spirit of wild nature. Much less Aphrodite, goddess of eros, of sexual union, the inspirer of love, who brought together bull and cow, stallion and mare, man and woman, in joyful and life–producing embrace. Her ways were far too devious and too much at variance with the spirit of Christian morality to be included in the Christian outlook. These neglected and rejected gods and goddesses, and the psychological functions they personify, have been the object of Christian repression and have reappeared in post–biblical art and folklore as the devil.

For this reason the devil is feared, for we fear what we have repressed, and we feel anxious in the face of those repressed elements within us that are struggling to reassert themselves. Small wonder that the devil constantly disturbs our peace of mind and disrupts our conscious state, for that which is repressed and denied throws the conscious status quo into confusion when it reemerges.

Yet, looked at from the psychological point of view we can see that the devil, in this sense of his meaning, appears to be a relative evil. If the devil personifies what has been rejected and denied, then the apparent evil with which he is surrounded could be dispelled if the repressed and rejected elements were reaccepted into consciousness. A split–off part of the psyche does indeed act in a devilish way. It has a disturbing effect upon consciousness, and, should it possess us entirely, it would be destructive. Moreover, if it is too split off, the rejected psychic content seems to fall into the hands of a deeper darkness and substrata of evil so that it acts for all the world like an evil power. Yet the task is always to redeem the lost part, to win it back from its alienated or evil state and reclaim it as part of the whole. Historically, Christianity has failed to see that its task is to win back, not to reject, these lost parts of ourselves devilish though they may seem to be. We try to exorcise, via repression, projection upon others, and various forms of denial and magic, what should not be exorcised but made conscious and integrated. Only then will the split–off parts of ourselves, the lost deities, cease to have their disturbing effects.

Thus the redemption of the devil is an important psychological task, for we cannot be whole without winning back the lost parts of ourselves. However troublesome Dionysus, Pan, and Aphrodite might be to the conventional Christian attitude, they, too, are part of human wholeness. They are not evil in themselves but add the color, vitality, and eros that we need in order to be whole people.

This may be what Origen had in mind many centuries ago when he spoke of the need for the ultimate redemption of the devil, a teaching we have already briefly mentioned in Chapter Four. At the end of history, Origen said, the devil, too, would be saved, for if the devil was not saved, then God's original creation would not be whole. After all, Origen stated, the devil was part of God's creation and plan, and so at the end, after his troublesome but necessary role as the disturber of man's consciousness was over, the devil would also be won back to the wholeness of God. But Origen's view was not popular with the Church, and finally he was condemned for this teaching in a council of the Church held in the sixth century.[8]

It is primarily the devil in this sense of the word that Jung says must be included as the *fourth* in order for wholeness to emerge. Jung often contrasts the Trinitarian aspect of Christian theology with the Quaternian symbols of wholeness that are produced by the unconscious. That is, while Christianity represents God as having a Triune nature, Father, Son, and Holy Ghost, the unconscious, through dreams, myths, and visions, spontaneously represents wholeness as having a four–fold structure. Thus Jung feels that insofar as our image of God is a representation of wholeness, the Christian symbol is incomplete. It lacks something because of its threeness, and a fourth must be added to make it complete. This fourth is the devil. This means that for wholeness to emerge, the unconscious, which contains all that has been repressed and thus made devilish, must also be included in our outlook. Only when the three becomes four can we become whole.

Sometimes the missing fourth is characterized by Jung as a masculine devil–image, sometimes he describes it as the fourth or inferior psychological function, but at other times the missing fourth is represented as the feminine, for it is the feminine side of life that has largely been rejected by an overly masculine, light–dominated, order–seeking consciousness. To be sure, the light, positive, more acceptable side of the feminine has been included in Roman Catholicism in the imagery of the Virgin Mary, but the earthy, eros, Yin side has been rejected, and Protestantism is devoid of even that. So the fourth is often represented as the missing feminine spirit of the psyche which, having been rjected, has turned witchlike in modern man, troubles his life and his conscience, and casts a bad spell on him because it has become vindictive.

This feminine spirit is associated with the world and the flesh, for the earth is the domain of the Great Mother. The ancient Baptismal formula of the Church, which goes back at least as far as the third century, calls for the priest to ask the would–be initiant into the faith: "Do you reject the world, the flesh, and the devil?" Thus the world and the flesh are connected with evil, though for what reason is not too clear, since the world and the flesh are both said to be part of God's plan and creation. It is, in fact, not Christianity at all that associates the world and the flesh with evil, but Gnosticism. Christianity is an incarnational religion, a religion that declares that God incarnated Himself in the flesh–"And the Word became Flesh" St. John's Gospel tells us. And it is Gnosticism that divided the creation in two and said that spirit was good and matter was evil, and that God reigned only in heaven while the evil demiurge presided over earth.

The Gnostic attitude, rejected theologically by the Church after centuries of theological struggle and debate, won the day after all by conquering Christian psychology and ethics. This can be seen in the traditional Christian attitude toward sexual life and pleasure, an attitude that said that sex was to be indulged in only for the purposes of procreation. In fact, even then, St. Augustine declared that it was a sin if one enjoyed it.[9] The idea that sexual pleasure might have a place in God's plan as a way of expressing love and relationship, a form of physical intimacy to accompany psychological intimacy, or even just for the sake of having a good time and expressing the joyfulness of life, was rejected as of the devil because, Gnostic fashion, the body was evil.

This rejection of the feminine spirit can be seen in the fascinating post–biblical legend of Lilith, the first woman, and later the wife of Satan, whose name means literally "belonging to the night."

The legend of Lilith is based on two biblical verses. Isaiah 34:14 says the place to be inhabited by Edom, defeated enemy of Israel,

> *Wild cats will meet hyenas there,*
> *the satyrs will call to each other,*
> *there too will Lilith take cover*
> *seeking rest.*

The second, and more important, biblical reference is found in Genesis 1:26 where we read: God said, "Let us make man in our own image, in the likeness of ourselves, and let them be masters of the fish of the sea, the birds of heaven, the cattle, all the wild beasts and all the reptiles that crawl upon the earth."

> *God created man in the image of himself,*
> *in the image of God he created him,*
> *male and female he created them.*

This verse implies that when God first created mankind he created male and female. He did not, as in the story we find in Genesis 2, create first the man Adam, and then as a second thought, the woman Eve.

The legend of Lilith goes back to this verse. Whatever became of the first woman God created? (Not Eve, but the *first* woman, alluded to in the above quotation.) Jewish sources, primarily, answer this question for us, the oldest of these being the Alphabet of Ben Sira, and the legend being later elaborated in the Talmud, the Targum, and the Cabala. According to Jewish legend, the trouble began because the first woman, Lilith, would not be subservient to Adam. (Evidently she was the first woman's liberationist.) Because she would not obey Adam, they quarreled, for Lilith claimed equal rights with Adam to be the chief of the family. But God sided with Adam, and Lilith was cast out of Eden, and it was then that God created Eve out of Adam's rib to take the place of Lilith as his wife. Not only was Lilith exiled, she was also cursed and made barren.

For a long time Lilith wandered about crying and feeling rejected until she encountered Samael, chief of the fallen angels, that is the devil, and she then became his wife. (It would seem that Samael was more open to the equality of the sexes.) Like a rejected feminine spirit, Lilith turned dark and planned revenge, and she and Samael plotted together against mankind, and conspired to drive Adam and Eve out of the Garden of Eden. This is why the serpent was slipped into the Garden of Eden. In fact, Christian writers who shared the story of Lilith with their Jewish contemporaries sometimes said that the serpent in the Garden was Lilith and not the devil.

Even though Adam and Eve were driven from the Garden they were not destroyed completely, thanks to God's saving action, and so Lilith's revenge was not complete, nor was her agony of soul appeased. So she became the enemy of mortal women and their children, a hag spirit of the night who tried to destroy newborn babies and tiny infants out of envy and revenge. And yet it was sometimes said that she did not want to destroy the children but only to embrace and hug them.

Here again we see the psychological truth exemplified: what we have rejected turns against us. In this case, it is the feminine spirit that has been denied, repressed, and rejected and which consequently turns into an evil spirit. And yet, if the process were reversed, and that which was rejected were loved and won back, then would it not leave the domain of evil and return to the good? Moreover, can we become whole without it? Certainly in this time of history it *is* the feminine spirit, the dark Yin power, which has been denied and rejected in men and in women, that now troubles our sleep and disturbs our souls, but which alone can make us whole by being included once again within the circle of our recognition, love, and acceptance.

That the devil personifies that which is feared and repressed is shown in other representations that have been in vogue at one time or another. For instance, during the Middle Ages the devil was associated with human reason. Rational thinking, the new scientific method that was just beginning to emerge, and the attempt to investigate and understand the secrets of nature were pictured by the Church as the devil's work. The devil was even personified as a famous scholar, and discoveries such as those of Galileo, which contradicted traditional ecclesiastical beliefs, were said to be the work of Satan. Clearly these new discoveries, and the new thinking attitude and scientific method that spawned them, were threats to the old faith and the security of entrenched consciousness. These threats brought with them the possibility of an inundation by the unconscious, since the ego always builds a wall of defense against the unconscious and regards anything that threatens this defense as evil. Again we see the truth: what we do not understand we tend to fear, and what we fear we tend to repress, and what we repress is the devil to us.

Later, when Puritanism became the vogue in England and parts of northern Europe, the devil was portrayed as an artist or musician who seduced mankind into these forms of creativity or play. It was said that the devil was particularly good at dancing, and that he might appear as a young man and so intrigue a young girl with his dancing that he would dance and dance with her until she collapsed and then he could carry her off. The Puritans, of course, did not so much repress reason as they did the Dionysian and pleasurable side of life. For them it was this side of life that reappeared in their fear of the dancing devil. Once again we see the psychological truth exemplified, that what is denied tends to return as a dark power.

The devil in folklore is also omnipresent. One never knows when he may be lurking about. Of course this is because the unconscious is also omnipresent. We may repress certain things we do not understand and fear, but we cannot escape them. They follow us wherever we go because, in the final analysis, they *are* us. So the devil too is inescapable and one must constantly be on guard against him.

Another reason for the omnipresence of the devil is that everything in the unconscious that has been repressed strives for reunion with consciousness. It is as though we put certain things in the basement of our house and shut the door tightly. But these things do not want to remain in the basement. They turn into devils and rattle the door and seek to find some way out of their imprisoned state and back into the world of consciousness. In so doing they create anxiety, since we tend to fear the return of the repressed. But this attempt of repressed contents to reach consciousness is not simply an attempt to disturb consciousness or gain revenge. The movement is toward the light of consciousness because this is necessary if psychological redemption is to occur. No matter how malignant these split–off contents of the psyche may appear to be, and no matter how malicious their tricks, there is always the possibility of their redemption if they can reach consciousness. Paradoxically, the redemption of these lost parts of ourselves also results in *our* redemption. That is, we can be whole only when we have helped redeem our devils.

The push of the devilish repressed psychic contents toward consciousness can be seen to be part of the thrust toward individuation, because we need to include these split–off parts of ourselves if we are to become whole. When there is too great a split in the psyche, the internal condition is represented as war, and a dangerous situation is the result. For if consciousness is overcome, there is the danger of an *enantiodromia*, that is, a running over from one opposite to another. If the devils we have repressed take over consciousness, that is not integration, but a defeat for the ego. Wholeness can only emerge when both sides of the coin are represented in consciousness at the same time; when we remain conscious of both our light and our dark sides.

Small wonder, then, that the devil is feared. And yet there is a curious aspect of this devil that appears in popular folklore, and that is his trustworthiness. This is seen in the famous "devil–compact" stories. In these tales a human being makes an agreement with the devil, usually to get the devil's aid in achieving some purpose. The interesting thing about these stories is that the devil can be tricked, because he always keeps his word and lives up to his agreement, but the human partner is free to deceive him if he has a chance. Or, Divine Powers may intercede, which are not bound by the terms of the contract, and they trick the devil at the last moment. As though it is recognized that the devil's word can be trusted, but that of his human partners cannot, the human being in these contracts must always sign his name in blood, but the devil's word alone is good.

The Theophilus legend of the sixteenth century is a good example. Theophilus was a highly esteemed cleric who was offered a bishopric but declined it out of modesty. But the new bishop, jealous of Theophilus' popularity, and resentful of his becoming Christian modesty, deprived him of his position in the Church. In order to recover his position Theophilus entered into a pact with the devil and agreed, in return for the devil's help, to deny Christ and the Virgin. The next day Theophilus was reinstated. When the end of his life approached Theophilus, aware of his dubious pact with the devil, fasted and prayed to the Virgin for pardon for forty days and forty nights. At last she relented, secured the document from the devil that Theophilus had signed with him, and consigned it to the fire. So in the end the devil was tricked, though he kept his word and got Theophilus the goal he wanted.

Such legends developed into the famous *Faust* story, which reached its culmination in Goethe's famous poem by that name. In this tale, too, the devil kept his word, and Mephistopheles did all that Faust wanted and commanded. But at the very end, as Mephistopheles waited for the soul of Faust to leave his body at death so he could take it to hell, the angels sent divine cherubs down to scatter rose petals over the scene. Mephistopheles was momentarily distracted by the erotic shower of roses and the charming cherubs, and in that instant Faust's soul left his body and was taken up by the angels to heaven. So the devil was cheated again.

Such stories hint at the fact that although the repressed contents of the unconscious can appear diabolical, and are indeed dangerous, they have their own kind of integrity, while the ego can cheat on the process of individuation.

This is a good place to pause and reassess where we are in our survey of the problem of evil. We have, in fact, been looking at many different aspects of what is, or appears to be, evil.

First we saw that what appears to be an adversary and an evil force can sometimes properly be called the dark side of the Self. That is, when human consciousness pits itself against Divine Wholeness, it inevitably constellates the dark side of God that confronts it as a dangerous, and even destructive, adversary. We saw this exemplified in the Old Testament story of Balaam. This dark power, however, no matter how destructive it can be, cannot be said to be intrinsically evil. To the contrary, a positive good may come from such a confrontation, and an advance in consciousness might be made through such an encounter that could be made in no other way. Even the destruction that the dark side of the Self may bring about can be considered good in the sense that it destroys that which is not worthy of living.

Second, we saw that the view of evil in the Gospels implies that evil is necessary for some Divine Purpose, and we noted that psychology supports this notion because it sees that without evil the developmental process we call individuation, with its growth of consciousness, could not take place. According to this view, while evil really is evil, there is nevertheless an overriding Purpose which it must serve.

Third, we saw that the problem of evil and the devil is complicated by the problem of the human Shadow. There is inevitably a part of us that resists the demand of consciousness to be perfect, to be entirely light, to have no sins, no failings, no reprehensible thoughts, fantasies, or impulses. This is the shadow personality. This shadow personality can look like evil, it can even act evil when it is split off too far from the whole. But in itself it cannot be said to be entirely evil, for if made conscious, recognized, and accepted, the Shadow loses its seemingly satanic character and even has the capacity to add to the stature, strength, and breadth of one's personality.

Fourth we saw that the devil is a personification of the power drive of the ego. There is within us something that wants to set the ego up against the Self, the human against the Divine Will. Legend personified this as Lucifer, whose power drive led to his expulsion from heaven. Here at last we may suppose we have a definite evil, but even here one suspects that unless such a power drive were present, the entire process of redemption could not take place. Psychologically speaking, this means that a certain power drive is necessary if the ego is to differentiate itself sufficiently to eventually experience a confrontation and reconciliation with God.

Finally we have seen that the devil can be a figure who personifies what has been repressed because it did not fit into the ideals or beliefs of the prevailing consciousness. In this case the devil becomes a kind of collective shadow figure, a figure whose darkness compensates a too rigid and one-sided conscious attitude. But in spite of the malicious, and even fearful tricks that such an alienated and split-off power can incite, the darkness with which the devil figure is surrounded must be said to be a relative evil since it changes when it is integrated.

A relative evil can be defined as an apparent evil which, under certain circumstances, can be changed for the better, or which can be said to be necessary for the purpose of a higher good. That which is intrinsically evil, on the other hand, would be a power that works for sheer destructiveness and is incapable of being altered from its evil state. So far our investigation of evil has shown that much of the evil we encounter is, in the final analysis, a relative evil. However, the story of Jekyll and Hyde suggested that there is an intrinsic or achetypal evil, since the further Hyde's personality absorbed Jekyll's the more sheer destructiveness was manifested. Clearly we need to look more deeply into the ontology of evil, and that is the subject we will undertake in the next chapter.

Notes

1 Origen, *De Principis*, Book I, Chapter V.

2 Archelaus, *The Disputation with Manes.* Ante-Nicene Fathers, Eerdmans Series, p. 205.

3 John 14:30. Cf. 12:31 and 16:11.

4 Maximilian Rudwin, *The Devil in Legend and Literature* (La Salle, Ill.: Open Court Publishing Company, 1973).

5 Matt. 4:1–11.

6 2 Cor. 11:14.

7 Stewart Farrar, *What Witches Do* (New York, N.Y.: Coward, McCann & Geoghagan, Inc., 1971), p. 31.

8 Some authorities say this condemnation was made in the year 553 at the Fifth Council of Constantinople, but others that it occurred in the year 543 at a local council in that city. Cf. Philip Schaff, *History of the Christian Church*, Vol. II, p. 791 (Grand Rapids, Mich.: Wm. B. Eerdmans Publishing Co., 1963. Reproduced by special arrangement with the original publisher, Chas. Scribners Sons, 1910).

9 Cf. *City of God*, Book XIV, chs. 16, 17, and 23, 24, and Book XVI, ch. 25.

CHAPTER NINE

The Ontology of Evil

The Problem of Evil
in Early Christianity

The problem of evil is unresolved in Christian theology. The main thrust of thought in the early Church was directed to the nature of Christ, how it was that Christ saved man, and the relationship of Christ to God the Father. Christology so took over the center of the stage that the discussion of evil and the relationship of evil to God was largely put aside. So it is that to this day there is no definitive statement about the nature of evil in the Christian creeds, nor is there any official Christian doctrine of evil.

However, while the early Church did not concentrate its energies on resolving the problem of evil, neither did it disregard it entirely. As we have already seen, the reality of evil was a primary concern in the Gospels, and also in the minds of persons in the early Church. So aware was the early Church of the reality of evil, in fact, that the first theories of the Atonement were couched in terms of it. How was it that Christ's death on the Cross saved mankind and enabled man to be again at–one with God? This was a great question with which the Church wrestled, and its first explanation was that Christ's death on the Cross saved man from the devil and the power of evil.

There were two theories of the Atonement along this line: the *ransom* theory and the *victory* theory. According to the first, Christ's death ransomed man back from the power of the devil. According to the second, Christ on the Cross vanquished the powers of evil and thus freed man from evil's power.

The ransom theory said that the devil had gained power over man's soul by tempting him to sin. This was originally done in the Garden of Eden by the devil who appeared in the form of the snake. Because of man's sin, his soul was now the devil's prisoner. But God decided to save man by offering the devil His Son, Christ, as a ransom for mankind. If the devil would release man, God would give him His Son instead. It was, however, a ruse, for Christ was perfect and blameless, and thus the devil could not hold him. God evidently felt it was fair to resort to a ruse in dealing with the devil inasmuch as the devil had also resorted to a ruse in order to gain power over man via the original temptation in the Garden of Eden.

The ransom theory was popular in the early Christian Church and held a prominent position for many centuries. Origen, Gregory of Nyssa, and Irenaeus subscribed to it in the East, while in the West it was the primary theory of the Atonement held by Augustine and Gregory the Great. Even as late as the twelfth century we find it represented in the thinking of Bernard of Clairvaux and Peter Lombard. It was Gregory the Great, for instance, who said Christ's humanity was the bait that caused the devil to bite on the hook of the Cross and thereby be snared, and Peter Lombard who compared the Cross with a mousetrap baited with Christ's blood.[1] The ransom theory was, and still is, an especially popular theory in the Greek Church, for among the Eastern Christians Satan and his demonic host were very real powers, and supernatural aid was deemed essential if mankind was not to be destroyed by them. No doubt much of the strength of this theory came from experiences of those Christians who felt that Christ had in fact defeated evil and thus made their lives possible.

In the Gospels, two scriptural passages are cited as the bases for the ransom theory: Matthew 20:27–28 which reads, "Anyone who wants to be first among you must be your slave, just as the Son of Man came not to be served but to serve, and to give his life as a ransom for many." The Greek word rendered *ransom* is *lytron*, which means literally a price paid for the purpose of redemption. A person might, for instance, pay a *lytron* in order to redeem a slave from servitude. Passages from the epistles cited in support of this idea include 1 Corinthians 6:20 and 7:23; 1 Peter 1:18f; Titus 2:14; and Ephesians 1:14.

The victory theory is like the ransom theory in that the devil is vanquished by Christ on the Cross, but there is less emphasis upon man's guilt and the need for a ransom, and more emphasis upon the cosmic struggle between Christ and Satan, a struggle ending in the victory of Christ via the Crucifixion. The Cross is thus the battleground between Christ and Satan, the seat of a cosmic struggle between the forces of God and the forces of evil. It was a favorite idea for Origen, who held it conjointly with the ransom theory, and who spoke of Christ triumphing over the principalities and powers, making a show of them, and overcoming them by His Cross.[2]

It was also this theory of the Atonement that was the basis for Christian exorcism. It was used, for instance, by Lactantius who, in *The Divine Institutes*, describes the power of the Cross to expel demons, and thus free men's souls and bodies from the power of evil.[3] In fact, to this day, whenever we make some positive statement about a piece of good fortune, and then superstitiously or piously knock on wood, we are acknowledging the victory of Christ over Satan on the Cross. For the wood on which we knock stands for the wood of the Cross which has the power to dispel Satan, who might otherwise hear what we have said and come and take away from us our bit of good luck. Scriptural references for this theory were found in the early Church in Colossians 2:15, Hebrews 2:14, and 1 John 3:8.

So prevalent were these early theories of the Atonement, couched in terms of the reality of evil, that it was not until St. Anselm (1033–1109) wrote his book *Cur Deus Homo*, that the ransom and victory theories were generally superceded by what has come to be known as the *satisfacion* or *penal substitutionary* theory. According to this view, it was not the devil who had to be satisfied, but God; Adam's sin had not placed man in the hands of the devil, but had been an offense against God; therefore it was God's justice that had to be satisfied. But sinful mankind could never atone for his sin before Almighty God, so God Himself offered up a sacrifice for man's sin in the person of Christ on the Cross. So Christ paid the debt for man, and this satisfied God's demand for justice.

The important point for our purposes is the emphasis placed in the early Church on evil, which was so real to the early Christians that the mission of Christ was defined in terms of it. One reason, in fact, for the success of Anselm's satisfaction or penal substitutionary theory of the Atonement was that the earlier theories seemed to give *too* much weight to evil, and seemed to set the devil up as such a powerful rival to God that God had to resort to what appeared to be a ruse in order to free man. Proponents of the victory theory no doubt would have asserted that the Atonement was no mere trick, but the assertion of Utimate Reality—which has the power to vanquish evil.

But of course none of this explained the origin or nature of evil. If there was only one God, and if God was just and good, and if God loved mankind and created a good world, why was there so much evil in the world? And did God simply allow this evil, or had He created the evil deliberately? What, after all, was the ultimate place of evil in the Divine Scheme of things? These were questions with which the early Church occasionally wrestled, but did not solve.

We have seen that in the Old Testament evil could be laid at God's door without a feeling of contradiction. But as man's conscience sharpened, and as man's image of God emphasized God's loving qualities and justice, it was no longer possible to say that God was the author of evil as well as good unless some explanation was given that could resolve the apparent contradictions that such a statement would create.

Various solutions were tried. One line of thought was that the origin of evil lay in man, not in God. It was man, after all, who had succumbed to the temptations in the Garden of Eden, and with this, evil entered into God's otherwise perfect creation. True, man was God's very own creation, and one might ask why God would have created such a weak creature, but the answer was that if man was to be what he was meant to be, he had to have free will, and this meant the capacity to choose evil as well as to choose good. According to this view, *Omne bonum a Deo, omne malus ab hominem*—all good to God and all evil from man.

This solution to the problem of evil was stated frequently in the early Church, and had the merit of absolving God of any responsibility for evil—or seemingly so. But in another sense it merely pushed the question back a step, for who, after all, had put the serpent in the Garden of Eden? Who was responsible for a creation that placed such an evil temptation in front of man, a creature notoriously weak in the moral realm? Moreover, it made man a co-creator with God, for if man created evil by his free will, then he was a creator of sorts in his own right. Moreover, it did nothing to explain the existence of natural evils, such as diseases, earthquakes, violent storms and other calamities that were brought about by nature and not by man's moral choice.

A second attempt to solve the problem of evil was the teaching that God deliberately allowed evil in His creation in order to create a universe in which man's moral powers could be exercised, and man's soul purged, cleansed, and developed. According to this view, without evil there would not be a world in which man's nature could be perfected. A leading proponent of this view was the Bishop of Lyon, Irenaeus, who regarded the fall of man as a blessing that was essential for man's development to perfection. "The original destination of man was not abrogated by the fall, the truth rather being that the fall was intended as a means of leading men to attain this perfection to which they were destined." [4]

Origen, as we have seen, was also a proponent of this point of view. God allowed evil, Origen said, because without evil to struggle against, the human soul could not properly develop. In fact, the devil himself was so much a part of God's plan that he too would be saved when the Divine Drama was finally concluded at the end of time and all the creation won back to unity with God. Evil would then cease to exist because it would no longer be necessary.

Lactantius likewise accepted the necessity of evil for the purpose of a higher good:

> For God designed that there should be this distinction between good and evil things, that we may know from that which is evil the quality of the good, and also the quality of the evil from the good; nor can the nature of the one be understood if the other is taken away. God therefore did not exclude evil, that the nature of virtue might be evident. How could patient endurance retain its meaning and name if there were nothing which we were compelled to endure? How could faith devoted to its God deserve praise, unless there were someone who wished to turn us away from God? For on this account He permitted the unjust to be more powerful, that they might be able to compel to evil; and on that account to be more numerous, that virtue might be precious, because it is rare. [5]

As a final example of this point of view in the early Church I quote from the *Recognitions* of Clement, an early Christian document of unknown origin, but commonly ascribed to Clement, Bishop of Rome, and from the *Clementine Homilies*, by the same author. Clement argued that God has two hands with which to accomplish His purpose, one good and one evil, and that there are two kingdoms that correspond to these two sides of God, one a kingdom of heaven and the other a kingdom of earth, with two kings over these kingdoms. "These two leaders," he says, "are the swift hands of God, eager to anticipate Him so as to accomplish His will." He cites Deuteronomy 32:39, "I will kill and I will make alive; I will strike, and I will heal," as evidence of these two hands of God, and goes on to say, "He kills through the left hand, that is, through the evil one, who has been so composed as to rejoice in afflicting the impious. And He serves and benefits through the right hand, that is, through the good one, who has been made to rejoice in the good deeds and salvation of the righteous. Now these have not their primary substance outside of God: for there is no other primal source."

That God's ultimate intentions, however, are for the good is indicated by Clement's eschatological view, which resembles Origen's, for Clement suggests that at the end of all things the principle of evil will be transformed, since it will no longer be necessary: "The Wicked one, then, having served God blamelessly to the end of the present world, can become good by a change in his composition." [6]

Clement's basic optimism about the ultimate goodness of God is also reflected in the fact that while the earthly realm is given over to evil, the heavenly realm is reserved for good: "God appointed two kingdoms and two ages, determining that the present world should be given over to evil, because it is small and passes quickly away. But he promised to preserve the future world for good, because it is great and eternal." [7]

The Doctrine of the *Privatio Boni*

There was another approach to the problem of evil, propounded by Christian thinkers, that received much attention from Jung: the doctrine of the *privatio boni*. Aristotle was the first to suggest this idea in his *Metaphysics* where he said that evil was

untruth and so did not exist in itself. In the Church this idea
became known as the *privatio boni* (deprivation of the good) and
originated with Origen. It soon found representation in Basil of
Caesarea, Dionysius the Areopagite, St. Augustine, and many
others, including Thomas Aquinas. The basic idea of the doctrine
of the *privatio boni* is that the good alone has substance, and that
evil has no substance of its own, but exists by means of a diminution of the good.

For instance, Origen called evil "the accidental lack of perfection." In other words, evil came into being as the creation fell
away from the perfection God intended for it. As we have already
seen, however, Origen also saw evil as part of God's total plan and
thought that the devil would ultimately be redeemed.

The influential Eastern theologian, Basil of Caesarea, says, "For
evil is the privation of good . . . And thus evil does not inhere in its
own substance, but arises from the mutilation of the soul." [8] The
Greek words translated "privation" and "mutilation" are *sterēsis*
and *promasin*. The former also means "loss," and the latter comes
from the Greek verb *pēráo*, meaning to maim or disable. Therefore the thought is that evil is a loss of goodness, that it has no
substance in its own right, but occurs through a maiming or
disabling of the perfection of the soul.

St. Augustine perhaps elaborated the doctrine of the *privatio
boni* more than any other Christian thinker. He did so, as we saw
in Chapter Two, in reaction to Mani, the Persian religious
philosopher whose attempt to resolve the problem of evil resulted
in Dualism. It was Augustine's difficult task to maintain Christian
monotheism and the Christian insistence on the goodness of the
world and its creation by God, and at the same time to account
for the existence of evil without laying the blame for it at the
doorstep of God or making evil a principle co–equal with God. In
attempting to resolve the problem Augustine resorted to the doctrine of the *privatio boni*, declaring in his *Confessions*, ". . . because as yet I knew not that evil was naught but a privation of
good, until in the end it ceased to be altogether." [9] Evil, according
to Augustine, would cease to be in the end, because ultimately
God's plan for creation would be perfectly fulfilled. Since evil
exists because of the loss of this fulfillment, evil by definition
would therefore cease to exist when the creation is fulfilled.

Jung's Criticisms of the *Privatio Boni*

The doctrine of the *privatio boni* has been attacked by Jung, who has subjected it to searching criticism. As we have seen, the doctrine of the *privatio boni* is not an official Christian teaching about evil and is only one of several approaches to the problem that can be found among Christian thinkers. Therefore Jung is not quite correct when he says, "According to the teachings of the Church, evil is simply 'the accidental lack of perfection,' " [10] since there is no single teaching of the Church in this regard. Nevertheless, Jung's criticisms of the doctrine are important, and deserve careful scrutiny. They can be summarized as follows:

1. Because the *privatio boni* regards the principle of evil as insubstantial, and splits off evil from any integral relationship with the Godhead, the figure of Christ as presented in the dogma of the Church is necessarily one–sidedly light. Christ is only goodness, love, justice, and mercy; there is no hint of darkness or malice in him. As a result of this one–sidedness, the dark side appears in the figure of the Antichrist, a figure who compensates the one–sidedness of the Christ–image. Jung writes, "The Christ–symbol lacks wholeness in the modern psychological sense, since it does not include the dark side of things but specifically excludes it in the form of a Luciferian opponent." [11] And elsewhere he adds, "The dogmatic figure of Christ is so sublime and spotless that everything else turns dark beside it. It is, in fact, so one–sidedly perfect that it demands a psychic complement (i.e., the Antichrist) to restore the balance." [12] And again, "In the Christian concept . . . the archetype (of wholeness) is hopelessly split into two irreconcilable halves, leading ultimately to a metaphysical dualism—the final separation of the kingdom of heaven from the fiery world of the damned." [13]

Jung contrasts the one–sidedly light figure of Christ with the nature of the empirical Self as it appears in dreams, visions, and other symbols of the individuation process. It is in the nature of the Self, he notes, to unite the opposites, even the opposites of good and evil. "For in the self good and evil are indeed closer than identical twins!" [14] And, "In the empirical self, light and shadow form a paradoxical unity." [15] The idea is that wholeness, which is made possible by the archetype of the Self, combines all things into a paradoxical unity, both light and dark, male and female, good and evil. Because this unity is essential to the Self, when the figure of Christ, who carries for Western man the image of the Self, is one–sidedly light, the dark side must necessarily turn up somewhere, e.g., in the split–off image of the Antichrist. Jung says the Christian attitude could not contain the image of the Self as a union of the opposites because of its inability to accept paradoxes. "For the Christian neither God nor Christ could be a paradox; they had to have a single meaning, and this holds true to the present day." [16]

Elsewhere Jung writes, "The Self is a union of opposites *par excellence*, and this is where it differs essentially from the Christ–symbol. The androgyny of Christ is the utmost concession the Church has made to the problem of opposites. The opposition between light and good on the one hand and darkness and evil on the other is left in a state of open conflict, since Christ simply represents good, and his counterpart the devil, evil. This opposition is the real world problem which at present is still unsolved. The self, however, is absolutely paradoxical in that it represents in every respect thesis and antithesis, and at the same time synthesis." [17]

Thus Jung feels that the image of Christ as a symbol of wholeness is contradicted by the psychological fact that the Self is not one–sidedly light, as the Church has represented Christ to be, but combines light and dark into a paradoxical unity, and when metaphysics conflicts with the facts, there has to be an objection. Jung writes, "I have to get polemical when metaphysics encroaches on experience and interprets it in a way that is not justified empirically." [18]

2. Jung becomes somewhat heated in his attack on the *privatio boni* because he believes that the splitting off of evil from the Godhead has had practical and deleterious results for mankind. The compensating and split–off image of the Antichrist has resulted in the autonomy of the principle of evil. Evil is no longer related to the whole, but is free to act entirely on its own, with the result that evil victimizes mankind with disastrous results.

Now if it were true that evil is "nothing but the privation of good," this might not be so bad, for one would not expect a principle that has no substance in itself to have much power. But, in fact, this is not the case. To the contrary, evil is exceedingly real.

And Jung says a doctrine such as the *privatio boni*, which he feels tends to diminish evil's reality, does mankind a disservice. It is the failure to take evil seriously that created the tendency for people to fall prey to it, either by being possessed by evil and being a perpetrator of it, or by becoming a victim of it. Therefore, says Jung, human feeling is against the doctrine of the *privatio boni*, or any such doctrine that overlooks mankind's sufferings, and weakens man's psychological preparedness to recognize and deal with evil.

3. Finally, Jung finds a logical objection to the doctrine of the *privatio boni:* he notes that man is compelled to think in terms of good and evil, even though what is good and what is evil is a human judgment and we do not know what they are in themselves. He argues that we cannot think good without thinking evil. They are a "logically equivalent pair of opposites . . . From the empirical standpoint we cannot say more than this . . . we would have to assert that good and evil, being coexistent halves of a moral judgment, do not derive from one another but are always together. Evil, like good, belongs to the category of moral values." [19] And elsewhere, in one of his letters, he wrote, "On the practical level the *privatio boni* doctrine is morally dangerous, because it belittles and irrealizes Evil and thereby weakens the Good, because it deprives it of its necessary opposite: there is no white without black, no right without left, no above without below, no warm without cold, no truth without error, no light without darkness, etc. If Evil is an illusion, Good is necessarily illusory too. That is the reason why I hold that the *privatio boni* is illogical, irrational and even a nonsense." [20]

Thus Jung's argument against the *privatio boni* has three points to it: (1) That the one–sidedly light image of Christ is in contradiction to the fact that the Self is a combination of the opposites. (2) That the splitting off of evil from the Godhead has given to evil too much autonomy with disastrous results for mankind, especially since the doctrine of the *privatio boni* lulls mankind into a false sense of security by denying the reality of evil. Thus human feeling is against it. (3) The logical objection that if we say good is real we must also say evil is real, since good and evil are a "logically equivalent pair of opposites."

We have already noted that Jung felt the Trinitarian symbol for

the Godhead was incomplete, insofar as it is a symbol of wholeness, and that the symbol of the Quarternity was more representative of totality. We are now in a position to understand more
deeply why Jung felt this way.

Jung does not invent the symbol of the Quaternity for wholeness, but is able to show that it comes up spontaneously in the
symbols of the unconscious in order to represent the whole state.
Wholeness, therefore, seems to have a four–fold structure, since
the four appears over and over as a highly important number
symbolic of the foundation for totality. Thus we have the Four
Gospels in Christian lore, the importance of the number four in
American Indian ritual, the four directions of the compass, the
four corners of the square, the four functions of the psyche, and
many other manifestations of the number four as a number that
includes all that belongs to a total state. In theology, Jung argues,
the Trinitarian symbol lacks completeness because of its three–
fold structure, and what must be included to make a totality is
the missing dark side. As we have seen, this is variously represented as the devil, the feminine, or the missing fourth function,
all of which, from the Christian point of view, are rejected because they are not in accord with the one–sidedly light and masculine image of the Deity that Christianity has espoused.

The fact that the missing fourth that completes the Quaternity
is represented in various ways is a little confusing. For instance,
Jung writes: "In Eastern symbolism the square ... has the
character of the *yoni:* femininity. A man's unconscious is likewise
feminine and is personified by the anima. The anima also stands
for the 'inferior' function and for that reason frequently has a
shady character; in fact she sometimes stands for evil itself. She
is as a rule the *fourth* person. She is the dark and dreaded mater-
nal womb which is of an essentially ambivalent nature. The
Christian deity is one in three persons. The fourth person in the
heavenly drama is undoubtedly the devil. In the more harmless
psychological version he is merely the inferior function." [21]

The matter can be clarified, however, when we understand
Jung to be saying that until the unconscious is included, totality
cannot be represented. The unconscious, into which all that is
morally suspect and objectionable to Christian consciousness has
been placed, often appears in a dubious light. It sometimes is

represented (at least in man's consciousness) as the anima (a female figure), sometimes as the devil, and sometimes as the missing fourth function of the psyche. Hence the "missing fourth," i.e., the unconscious, can be represented by any of these three figures.

A Critique of Jung's View
of the *Privatio Boni*

Jung's position regarding the relationship of evil to God has not received the attention among Christian and other thinkers that it deserves. Nevertheless, it has not gone entirely unnoticed, and has received a careful review by at least one religious philosopher, H. L. Philp, who, in his book *Jung and the Problem of Evil* pays Jung the compliment of taking him seriously. Some of Philp's arguments are worth noting.

Philp rejects the idea that the Quaternity, as Jung understood it, can be taken as a symbolic representation of God, because it "enthrones evil forever." This, in his view, creates an amoral God, for if the Godhead itself is both good and evil, then, "Evil is inevitable and eternal and amorality is enthroned forever, for if goodness comes then evil cannot be far behind, and so the circle turns—for eternity." [22]

He points out that if, as Jung says, human feeling revolts against the idea that evil is insubstantial, it even more revolts against the idea that the Ultimate Source of Life, God, is inherently evil. In short, Philp finds Jung's idea that God contains good and evil repugnant from the human, feeling point of view, just as Jung finds the doctrine of the *privatio boni* repugnant from the feeling point of view because it seemingly declares that evil is unreal, thus seeming to make a mockery of human suffering.

Philp also tries to defeat Jung's argument that the doctrine of the *privatio boni* is illogical since good and evil are logical equivalents, so that to assert the existence of one is necessarily to posit the existence of the other. Not so, Philp argues, for not all qualities have their logical opposite. To be sure, outside implies inside, and up implies down, but the sun would be hot even if nothing were known about a colder condition. So too, he feels, we can posit the good without necessarily having to think of the evil.

Allan Anderson, Professor of Religious Studies at San Diego

State University, supports Philp's position in this regard.[23] Good and evil, he points out, are not logically equivalent opposites because they are to be understood not in terms of each other, but in terms of a norm. In this case, we decide what is good and what is evil when observing how the meaning of evil depends on the meaning of good.

The norm by which we determine what is good and what is evil, we can say, is the higher good of wholeness. Whatever detracts from or destroys wholeness we call evil, and whatever supports, furthers, or maintains wholeness we call good. We can think wholeness without having to think its opposite. According to this view, Jung erred in failing to see that both good and evil, as perceived from our human point of view, are to be defined in terms of a norm that is beyond them both.

In at least one place Jung himself seems to recognize that good and evil are to be defined in terms of some other norm. In *Aion* he writes, " 'Good' is what seems suitable, acceptable, or valuable from a *certain point of view;* evil is its opposite." [24] Here good and evil are determined from a "certain point of view," and this viewpoint suggests there is a norm which determines what is good and what is evil. From the egocentric human point of view this "norm" is, no doubt, what suits our pleasure, convenience, or plans. For instance, in the example we used earlier, the Puritan settlers in this country said it was good that a plague had rid the country of the Indians, but the Indians surely deemed that plague an evil, each judging what was good and evil in terms of the norm of personal desires. But from a larger point of view that norm could be a wholeness that lies beyond relative good and evil.

Jung also, at least occasionally, spoke of a goal toward which all life strives, in terms of which good and evil may be judged. This teleological view of good and evil is reflected in *Aion* where Jung says, "To strive after *teleōsis*—completion— . . . is not only legitimate but is inborn in man as a peculiarity which provides civilization with one of its strongest roots. This striving is so powerful, even, that it can turn into a passion that draws everything into its service." [25] But elsewhere, when Jung equates good and evil as a pair of opposites to be united in the Self, rather than as judgments devised by mankind in terms of the norm of wholeness, he departs from his teleological attitude.

Dr. Anderson also argues that the doctrine of the *privatio boni* does not deny the reality of evil but defines its nature. Jung, as we have seen, finds the doctrine repugnant because it "nullifies the reality of evil," [26] and declares that evil is "something that does not exist." [27] This is not so, says Anderson, for the doctrine of the *privatio boni* does not deny the reality of evil but states what evil is. It says that while evil exists it can only exist by living off the good and cannot exist on its own.

Now if the highest Good is wholeness, and if we say that the good is what promotes wholeness, and the evil is that which seeks to destroy wholeness, then we can see in what sense it is true that evil cannot exist on its own, even though it is real. Suppose that wholeness were perfectly established. Then there would be no basis for the existence of evil since there would no longer be anything destructive, everything being included in the whole. Or, suppose that wholeness were completely destroyed. Once again evil could not exist, for if there were no longer anything to destroy, evil would cease to be.

Consider the analogy of illness and health. We can argue that illness is a diminution (privation) of health, and that illness, while very real to human life, cannot exist on its own, but that does not deny its existence. If all living creatures were perfectly healthy, there would be no illness. And if an illness has succeeded in completely destroying a healthy organism, that illness also ceases to exist. For instance, if a person succumbs to a disease such as cholera, once the health of that person's body has been totally destroyed, the illness of cholera also ceases to exist there, for how can there be an illness except in a relatively healthy host? The cholera bacteria might continue to exist, but cholera bacteria are not an illness until they are activated in a healthy body. They do no harm until they are destroying an organism.

A Reformulation of the Problem of Evil

In the light of these considerations, let us see if we can reformulate the problem of evil in a way that takes into account both Jung's criticisms and the arguments against these criticisms.

But first we must clarify some terms. One thing that makes it difficult to come to grips with Jung's arguments regarding evil is that sometimes he does not define terms. This gives to the whole issue a certain slipperiness; we think we are catching hold of something and then it suddenly eludes us. For instance, Jung seems to use the terms dark and evil interchangeably and without regard for precise definitions of these terms. For instance, he speaks of "the opposition between light and good on the one hand and darkness and evil on the other." The dark and the light certainly seem to go together in order to make a whole, just as night and day belong together to complete a whole cycle, but this does not mean that evil and good coexist together in some eternal arrangement of wholeness. What is dark is not necessarily evil but may be the necessary complement to the light. In fact, we instinctively sense that dark and light *do* belong together, and that a world that was all light and all day, with no darkness and no night, would be intolerable. This sort of seduces us, then, into accepting the idea that evil belongs eternally with the good, but this is not necessarily so. "Shadow" is another word Jung uses without precise meaning. A Shadow is not necessarily evil, but Jung uses this word in a way that implies that it is. Neither, for that matter, is black necessarily evil, even though it is to be contrasted with white.

Even more important is the fact that Jung rarely draws clear distinctions between the different experiences of evil. The word evil appears throughout Jung's writings as though it always has a single meaning, yet, as we have seen, there are different experiences that we call evil, which we summarized at the end of the last chapter. For instance, the experience of the dark side of God or the Self cannot be said to be intrinsically evil because it has a certain purpose. Even though the dark side of God destroys, it only destroys that which is not fit to exist. The devil, too, as the personification of elements of the personality that have been repressed and denied, is only relatively evil, since these qualities can be redeemed and the evil is then altered. We have already noted that evil is intensified as a condition of dissociation is increased. Thus the Shadow, which we observed in our study of Jekyll and Hyde, seems to become more evil the more it is split off from consciousness and lives autonomously without regard for the whole. So there are conditions and degrees of evil, and to speak clearly these must be taken into account.

However, occasionally Jung does make distinctions between different experiences of evil. For instance, in *Aion* he says, "It is quite within the bounds of possibility for a man to recognize the *relative* evil of his nature, but it is a rare and shattering experience for him to gaze into the face of *absolute* evil." [28] Unfortunately, Jung does not elaborate on what he regards as the distinction between relative and absolute evil. But since something absolute exists entirely on its own, we must suppose that Jung means that there is an evil that is unconditioned by anything else. However, that would nullify the existence of the good, since one absolute rules out the other absolute. To say there is absolute evil means there can be no absolute good. To speak of absolute evil is like stating a doctrine of the *privatio* in reverse. One would then have to say that evil is absolute, and good is whatever diminished the evil, but that the good cannot exist on its own apart from the evil, for something is not absolute if its opposite has an equal existence.

However, we can regard Jung's above statement as having emotional meaning. That is, that in some cases we feel we are looking at something that is only relatively evil and therefore might be redeemed, and in some cases we are looking at something that is intrinsic evil and therefore has a more horrifying effect. In terms of the idea of the *privatio boni* an entity exhibits the qualities of intrinsic evil the more dissociated it is from the whole, yet intrinsic evil cannot exist apart from that which it seeks to destroy. In terms of the *privatio boni* only Wholeness (the Good) is absolute, and evil, while it may exist in either a relative or a more pure or intrinsic form, cannot exist apart from the wholeness it seeks to destroy.

Jung himself speaks of saving the world and man's soul through the assimilation and transformation of evil. For instance, in an interview with Mircea Eliade, held at the 1952 Eranos Conference, Jung stated, "The great problem in psychology is the integration of opposites. One finds this everywhere and at every level. In *Psychology and Alchemy* (CW 12) I had occasion to interest myself in the integration of Satan. For, as long as Satan is not integrated, the world is not healed and man is not saved. But

Satan represents evil, and how can evil be integrated? There is only one possibility: to assimilate it, that is to say, raise it to the level of consciousness. This is done by means of a very complicated symbolic process which is more or less identical with the psychological process of individuation." [29] Now, if evil can be assimilated and integrated, and thereby the world is healed, then clearly it cannot be an absolute, since one cannot change the nature of an absolute. Thus Jung here seems to be saying that evil is not absolute, but is relative, and that the relativity of evil is to be judged in terms of the norm of wholeness. This is exactly what the doctrine of the *privatio boni* is saying in slightly different language.

Jung justly criticizes the Church for neglecting the task of dealing with evil. Because the Church declined the task, it fell to alchemy and, in our time, to psychology to complete the work. Jung notes in one of his letters, "Historical Christian psychology thinks rather of suppression of evil than of a *complexio boni et mali*. Thus alchemy tried the idea of a certain transformation of evil with a view to its future integration. In this way it was rather a continuation of Origen's thought that even the devil may be ultimately redeemed." [30]

As mentioned previously, the idea of the transformation of evil suggests that there is indeed something called wholeness in terms of which evil is to be defined. In the case of Origen, however, it was not evil that was to be redeemed, but the devil, so the figure of the devil would be saved but not the evil within him. Thus the destructive effects of the devil would be nullified, but the devil, as a creature of God, in whom evil at one time resided, would be won back.

Let us now attempt to reformulate the situation with regard to evil. We can say that intrinsic evil is a force of destructiveness that destroys wholeness. However, that which is evil can be redeemed by being freed from a dissociated, destructive condition and won back to the whole. The process of psychological integration aims at this. We can say that something that is dissociated is relatively evil because its evil varies with its state of dissociation. Thus Hyde at first appeared to be only mischievous and fun-loving, but as the dissociation in Jekyll's personality increased

Hyde became increasingly pure evil. However, we cannot speak of an absolute evil unless we wish to subordinate the good to the evil.

It was because Jung seemed to assert that evil has an absolute existence that many people reject his ideas, like Philp, who rebels at what he regards as the enthronement of evil. Actually, I do not think that is what Jung meant. Jung meant that there is a genuinely evil condition that can be altered when that condition is transformed and its legitimate contents integrated into the whole. But since Jung is not very clear about this, and insists on speaking of evil as though it were an absolute, one can understand how the impression is given that Jung intended to enthrone an absolute evil as part of the Godhead.

That Jung did not believe God to be a combination of good and an absolute evil is shown, I believe, in his autobiography where he discusses God as love.[31] Like many others before him, Jung is unable to explain the mystery of love, but says that the realm of Eros escapes our rational understanding and rational modes of representation. He feels that St. Paul's words in 1 Corinthians 13 "say all there is to be said; nothing can be added to them." Jung states that "we are in the deepest sense the victims and instruments of cosmogonic 'love'" and that in "the sentence 'God is love,' the words affirm the *complexio oppositorum* of the Godhead." After all, this is not so very different from the Christian position expressed in the *privatio boni*. To say that God is a *Summum Bonum* or that God is a cosmogonic love is saying much the same thing. Nor does Jung feel that in affirming that God is love one must also affirm the opposite, that God must be hate as well. Evidently in this case Jung has no difficulty thinking love without at the same time positing hate as a logical opposite that must have an equally substantial existence.

The fact is that Jung is sometimes frustratingly inconsistent in his arguments regarding evil and God. His inconsistency would not be so difficult if it were not that at each point of his inconsistency he is quite adamant about his position.

Jung's Objections Reviewed

Now let us look again at Jung's objections to the doctrine of the *privatio boni* in the light of this reformulation. We will remember that Jung's objections lay in three areas. First, Jung felt that the doctrine declared that evil was insubstantial, therefore had no reality, and that this was an offense to human sensibilities since evil is experienced as all too real. We can now see that the doctrine of the *privatio boni,* properly undeestood, does not deny the reality of evil, but declares what evil is and under what conditions it exists. It does say, however, that evil cannot exist on its own. If, for instance, the power of evil were to triumph completely, all wholeness would be destroyed. But this would result in the destruction of evil as well, since as a power of destruction, evil can only exist by virtue of something to destroy.

This conclusion agrees with the *I Ching.*[32] Consider Hexagram 36, *Ming I–Darkening of the Light.* This hexagram depicts a situation in which the sun has sunk under the earth and so has been darkened, that is, a state in which the dark or evil power is in the ascendancy. The sixth line of this hexagram reads:

> *Not light but darkness,*
> *First he climbed up to heaven,*
> *Then he plunged into the depths of the earth.*

Richard Wilhelm, in his commentary on this line, says:

> Here the climax of the darkening is reached. The dark power at first held so high a place that it could wound all who were on the side of good and of the light. But in the end it perishes of its own darkness, *for evil must itself fall at the very moment when it has wholly overcome the good, and thus consumed the energy to which it owed its duration.* (Italics mine.)

We find a similar philosophy of evil in Hexagram 23, *Po–Splitting Apart.* In this hexagram an evil situation is developing as the dark lines are mounting upward to overthrow the last of the light lines by means of a disintegrating influence. The reading for the sixth line of this hexagram says:

> *There is a large fruit still uneaten.*
> *The superior man received a carriage.*
> *The house of the inferior man is split apart.*

Richard Wilhelm says of this line:

> Here the splitting apart reaches its end. When misfortune has
> spent itself, better times return. The seed of the good remains,
> and it is just when the fruit falls to the ground that good
> sprouts anew from its seed. The superior man again attains
> influence and effectiveness. He is supported by public opinion
> as if in a carriage. But the inferior man's wickedness is visited
> upon himself. His house is split apart. A law of nature is at work
> here. *Evil is not destructive to the good alone but inevitably de-
> stroys itself as well. For evil, which lives solely by negation, cannot
> continue to exist on its own strength alone.*

It is interesting to compare these quotations from the *I Ching*
with a statement from St. Augustine:

> Evil . . . can have no existence anywhere except in some good
> thing . . . So there can be things which are good without any
> evil in them, such as God himself, and the higher celestial be-
> ings; but there can be no evil things without good. For if evils
> cause no damage to anything, they are not evils; if they do
> damage something, they diminish its goodness; and if they
> damage it still more, it is because it still has some goodness
> which they diminish; and if they swallow it up altogether,
> nothing of its nature is left to be damaged. And so there will be
> no evil by which it can be damaged, since there is then no
> nature left whose goodness any damage can diminish.[33]

A second objection Jung had to the doctrine of the *privatio boni*
was that it contradicted the psychological facts. That is, symbols
of the Self include the dark as well as the light; they combine
good and evil into a paradoxical whole. The Self is not light, but
dark and light; not good, but good and evil all at once. This holds
true as long as we recognize that what is dark is not necessarily
evil, and that it is not evil that is included in the wholeness of the
Self since evil is, by definition, destructuve to wholeness. That
which is relatively evil performs in an evil, destructive way as
long as it is not included in the wholeness of things, but when
wholeness is operative then all things are united and destruction
ceases. In other words, the Self does include "the devil," as the
personification for what has hitherto been rejected but can ultimately belong to the whole. Jung is correct in saying that the

missing "fourth" is necessary if wholeness is to occur. But this is not to say that the power of evil is at the heart of the Self, or of the Divine Order that presumably lies beyond the empirical Self. For by its very nature the Self, as the archetype of wholeness, must exclude and negate the power of evil, which is a principle of destruction. Nor is there any empirical evidence that the Self has any of the attributes of evil. To the contrary, where the Self is manifested we find something of supreme value, a true *Summum Bonum*, and the power of evil is nullified.

Finally there was Jung's logical objection that to think good requires us also to think evil. We can now see that this is not necessarily the case, when by good we mean not the human judgment of what is good and evil, but the ultimate norm by which we evaluate what is good and what is evil. This norm can be called the Good (with a capital G) or Wholeness. It is clear that to think wholeness we do not have to think its opposite, just as we can feel, experience, and think health without thinking illness.

As we have seen, Jung had no inclination to involve himself in metaphysics, but felt impelled to do so because in the case of the *privatio boni* he felt that metaphysics was encroaching upon experience in a way that was not justified empirically. But I think we can now see that the doctrine of the *privatio boni* does not conflict with the empirical facts. Indeed, the *Summum Bonum* of the doctrine of the *privatio boni* looks very much like Jung's *Self* since the "Good" of the *privatio boni* refers to the perfect fulfillment of a purpose or function. Nevertheless, the doctrine does remain metaphysical. To say it is possible that there is a God Who is a *Summum Bonum* is not to prove that this is actually so. For no one can say they know what the Ultimate is. For all we know, perhaps all that exists is a world in which one force works for wholeness, and another force works against wholeness, and there is nothing beyond this. This is a point we must examine more carefully, but first let us look again at the Christian position with regard to evil in the light of what we have said, and then at certain corrections in the Christian attitude that Jung's position on evil makes imperative.

Another Look at the Christian Position

I have tried to show that the doctrine of the *privatio boni* is a defendable philosophical idea. Interestingly enough, this does not detract from the other early Christian attitudes toward evil that we have mentioned. For instance, the *privatio boni*, as we have noted, does not in any way detract from the reality of evil. As we have seen, the original Christian position found in the Gospels and early Church was so cognizant of its reality that its theory of the Atonement was couched in terms of the problem of evil.

Nor does the doctrine of the *privatio boni*, understood in the correct way, contradict the position taken up by Clement and others that evil is allowed by God in order to accomplish His purpose. If wholeness is the highest Good, and if this is to be accomplished, then everything that is created must perform its proper function. The proper function of the ego is to achieve consciousness. This would not seem to be possible without the activity of evil. It is only when we come up against evil that consciousness is raised to a certain height. So it may be, paradoxically, that God allows evil because, even though it seeks to destroy wholeness, wholeness in the spiritual sense would be impossible without it.

This position has already been summarized in statements referred to earlier. If this is so, it may even be that Origen is correct, and that at the end of history evil, too, will cease to exist, its proper function having been played out in the cosmic drama and therefore no longer necessary. We are left with the seemingly paradoxical statement by the Russian philosopher Nicholas Berdyaev: "It is equally true that a dark source of evil exists in the world and that in the final sense of the word there is no evil." [34]

Jung says very much the same thing. In a discussion of the role of the devil he writes:

> The question we are confronted with here is the independent position of a creature endowed with autonomy and eternality: the fallen angel. He is the fourth, "recalcitrant" figure in our symbolical series ... Just as, in the Timaeus, the adversary is the second half of the second pair of opposites, without whom the world-soul would not be whole and complete, so, too, the devil must be added to the *trias* as *to en tetarton* (the One as the Fourth), in order to make it a totality ... Through the intervention of the Holy Ghost, however, man is included in the divine process, and this means that the principle of separateness and autonomy over against God—which is personified in Lucifer as

the God-opposing will—is included in it too. But for this will there would have been no creation and no work of salvation either. The shadow and the opposing will are the necessary conditions for all actualization. An object that has no will of its own, capable, if need be, of opposing its creator, and with no qualities other than its creator's, such an object has no independent existence and is incapable of ethical decision. At best it is just a piece of clockwork which the Creator has to wind up to make it function. Therefore Lucifer was perhaps the one who best understood the divine will struggling to create a world and who carried out that will most faithfully. For, by rebelling against God, he became the active principle of a creation which opposed to God a counter-will of its own. Because God willed this, we are told in Genesis 3 that he gave man the power to will otherwise. Had he not done so, he would have created nothing but a machine, and then the incarnation and the redemption would never have come about.[35]

I have quoted Jung at length because it shows that he is actually very close to the original Christian thought regarding evil. It would be hard, for instance, to tell the difference between what Jung says here and what Irenaeus said about the blessedness of the fall of man, since because of it Christ's redemption could take place.

There remains, however, a basic optimism in the Christian attitude toward evil that we do not often hear in Jung. Without denying the reality of evil, nor overlooking the destructive power of evil and its dangers to mankind, the Christian symbol of the Crucifixion and Resurrection points to an ultimately optimistic conclusion to the Divine Drama. For the Resurrection symbolizes the ultimate indestructibility of wholeness. It is a way of saying that in the final analysis, no matter what the forces of evil do, the integrity of wholeness cannot be destroyed. That is why Christ rises again victoriously even after having been seemingly destroyed by the evil forces.

On the psychological level this would correspond to the indestructibility of the Self. It would be a way of saying that when the Self is realized, there is an invulnerability to the powers of evil; the destructive powers cannot destroy the realized Self. On the human level it means that if a human being is centered, and related to the Self, there is a certain protection against evil; and when the center of the personality is established, such a person is supported by a more–than–human strength to resist and overcome the evil powers.

This Christian optimism toward evil, however, is not based on an optimistic view of either human nature or of this world. Evil will not be overcome because people are good, nor because the world is or can ever be a good place. It can only be overcome by virtue of the superior power of God. Human nature remains all too vulnerable to influences of evil, and Jung is correct that we should not be too sanguine about it. And the world, insofar as we can foresee, will always remain an imperfect cauldron full of turmoil and trouble, but a world in which some individual persons might nevertheless achieve consciousness.

Again, we are talking the language of metaphysics. We cannot know scientifically what the Ultimate Plan of life is, or even if there is such an Ultimate Plan. At a certain point knowledge comes to an end, and faith must take over. The only empirical knowledge of these things we have is the psychological fact that *if* a person's life is grounded in the wholeness of the Self, then there does seem to be a certain permanence and indestructibility about it, and a protection that keeps that person's soul from succumbing to evil. And, who knows, such a soul may endure in a life beyond death as well.

Our argument now comes full circle, and paradox builds upon paradox. We have noted that evil may be necessary if wholeness is to come about since wholeness can only occur when all creatures perform their proper function, and it would seem that human moral and psychological consciousness can only develop in the face of evil. It may be, therefore, that even evil is part of God's plan. We are back to Clement's idea that God has a right and left hand with which to carry out His Will. Yet at the same time we say this, we also say that wholeness does not include evil, and that when wholeness is either established or destroyed, evil also ceases to be.

Yet it is correct that in this study of the ontology of evil we should find that the loose ends do not all come together, and that the final answer escapes us. The worst thing in the world might be to suppose that the problem of evil had been solved on either an intellectual or emotional level. It is better for us to be left wondering, with a hint, to be sure, about the relationship between evil and God, but with no final answer. For we are more apt to discover the truth as we contemplate God as the Great Mystery, instead of supposing that we have reduced God to a final truth we can understand in human terms.

I have tried to argue that the position of the *privatio boni* with regard to evil is possible and not inconsistent with the psychological facts. Nonetheless, Jung's work has made it imperative that the typical conventional stance toward evil evidenced by most Christians must be significantly altered.

For instance, when Jung says that our image of totality must shift from three to four he is psychologically correct insofar as this means there must be a shift away from an attitude based on a purely conscious position, to an attitude that includes the unconscious as well. This means the recognition and inclusion of the devil. As we have seen, this does not mean that intrinsic evil is accepted or "enthroned," as Philp would put it, but that the necessity for evil is accepted, and an attempt made to transform it. On the operational level, this means there must be an attempt to include and integrate into our conscious attitude all that belongs to our essential wholeness that has been rejected, split off, and repressed into the unconscious.

This process of integration cannot take place if the conscious attitude remains rigid, one–sided, and insistent on only the light side of things. Only if the dark side of life, and the dark side of the Self, is accepted, is this process possible. And its ultimate success can only come about if consciousness is willing to accept a paradoxical view of wholeness, and is willing to work out an individual, rather than collective solution to the problems of life and personality. In short, we can never be "perfect," that is, without spot, blemish, or imperfection, but we can move toward wholeness which is, as Jung says, a highly paradoxical state.

The traditional Christian attitude as it has been mediated through the Church has rejected too much. It has refused to accept the Shadow side of the personality, and has rejected the dark side of the Self. It has insisted upon an impossible standard of perfection, and has not acknowledged the necessity, even the value, of a wholeness that comes about through imperfection, not through perfection. In refusing to accept the paradoxical nature of totality it has specifically excluded the feminine aspect of life and personality. This has not brought about a state of light and perfection, but has increased evil by driving parts of the personality into a split–off state. The conventional Christian attitude must therefore turn itself about and see the necessity for the redemption of that which has fallen into the hands of evil, even though this involves a descent into the dangerous realm of the unconscious.

Notes

¹ Bernard, *Moralia* xxxiii–7; Peter Lombard, *Liber Sententiarum* III, Dist xix 1.

² Cf. Origen's *Commentary on John* (chapter 37).

³ For an interesting exorcism commandment couched in these terms, see Lactantius, *The Divine Institutes* (chapter L).

⁴ Harnack, *History of Dogma* (Vol. 2, p. 271). See especially Irenaeus' *Against Heresies*, bk. 4, chs. 37–39, and bk 3, ch. 20, from the *Ante-Nicene Fathers* (Wm. B. Eerdman Publishing Co., Vol. I, 1885).

⁵ Lactantius, *Divine Institutes* bk. 5, ch. 7.

⁶ *Clementine Homilies*, Homily 20, ch. 3. Cf. VIII 130, 179, 180, 183, 184. Cf. *Recognitions*. Vol. 8, 140.

⁷ Quoted by Jung in *Aion* CW 9,2 (New York, N.Y.: Pantheon Books, 1959), p. 55.

⁸ *Hexaemeron*, II, 5. Quoted by Jung, *Ibid*, pp. 46–47.

⁹ Augustine, *Confessions*, Book III, ch. vii—Eerdmann Series.

¹⁰ C. G. Jung, *Aion*, p. 41.

¹¹ *Ibid.*, p. 41.

¹² *Ibid.*, p. 42.

¹³ *Ibid.*, p. 42.

¹⁴ C. G. Jung, CW 12, *Psychology and Alchemy* (Princeton, N.J.: Princeton University Press, 1953), p. 21.

¹⁵ Jung, *Aion*, p. 42.

¹⁶ *Ibid.*, p. 46. This is a strange statement for Jung to make since original Christian theology is highly paradoxical. Christ as both fully human

and fully divine, the idea of a God who dies but rises, the thought of the heavenly power incarnating in the flesh—all of these are highly paradoxical thoughts.

[17] Jung, *Psychology and Alchemy*, p. 19.

[18] Jung, *Aion*, p. 54.

[19] *Ibid.*, p. 47.

[20] C. G. Jung, *Letters 2* (Princeton, N.J.: Princeton University Press, 1975), p. 61.

[21] Jung, *Psychology and Alchemy*, par. 192.

[22] H. L. Philp, *Jung and the Problem of Evil* (New York, N.Y.: Robert M. McBride Co., 1959), p. 43.

[23] In lectures and private conversations.

[24] Jung, *Aion* p. 53. (Italics are mine.)

[25] *Ibid.*, p. 69.

[26] *Ibid.*, p. 46.

[27] C. G. Jung, CW 14, *Mysterium Coniunctionis* (Princeton, N.J.: Princeton University Press, 1963), p. 79.

[28] Jung, *Aion*, par. 19. (Italics are mine.)

[29] R. F. C. Hull and William McGuire, eds., *C. G. Jung Speaking* (Princeton, N.J.: Princeton University Press, 1977), p. 227.

[30] Jung, *Letters 2*, p. 401. (Italics are Jung's).

[31] C. G. Jung, *Memories, Dreams, Reflections* (New York, N.Y.: Pantheon Books, 1961), Sec. 3, ch. 12, "Late Thoughts." I am indebted to my friend Morton T. Kelsey for reminding me of this relevant passage.

[32] Richard Wilhelm, Trans., *The I Ching* (New York, N.Y.: Pantheon Books, 1955, 3rd printing), pp. 153 and 102–103. (Italics are mine.)

[33] *Contra adversarium legis et prophetarum*, I, 4f, quoted by Jung in *Aion*, p. 50.

[34] Nicholas Berdyaev, "Meaning of the Creative Act," *Collier Books Edition*, 1962, p. 138.

[35] C. G. Jung, CW 11, *Psychology and Religion*, "A Psychological Approach to the Trinity," par. 290. (New York, N.Y.: Pantheon Books, second printing, 1963).

Index

Inasmuch as the principal subject in this book is evil, that word is not included in the index except for a few special entries.